Shining Lights

RenewedMinds, an imprint of Baker Academic, publishes quality textbooks and academic resources to guide readers in reflecting critically on contemporary issues of faith and learning. While focused on the needs of a Christian higher education curriculum, RenewedMinds resources will engage and benefit all thoughtful readers.

Shining Lights

A History of the Council for Christian Colleges & Universities

James A. Patterson

A RenewedMinds Book

 Baker Academic

A Division of Baker Book House Co
Grand Rapids, Michigan 49516

Published by Baker Academic
a division of Baker Book House Company
P.O. Box 6287, Grand Rapids, MI 49516-6287

Printed in the United States of America

Library of Congress Cataloging-in-Publication Data

Patterson, James A., 1947–
    Shining lights : a history of the Council for Christian Colleges & Universities / James A. Patterson.
      p.   cm.
    Includes bibliographical references.
    ISBN 0-8010-2264-9 (paper)
    1. Council for Christian Colleges & Universities. 2. Church colleges—United States. 3. Protestants—Education (Higher)—United States. I. Title.
LC538 .P38 2001
378′.071′0973—dc21
                                   00-045529

For information about academic books, resources for Christian leaders, and all new releases available from Baker Book House, visit our web site:
http://www.bakerbooks.com

To
Gordon Werkema,
John Dellenback,
Myron Augsburger,
Robert Andringa,
John Bernbaum,
Richard Gathro,
and Karen Longman,
all former or current leaders
who have made significant contributions
to the history of the Council
for Christian Colleges & Universities

Contents

Foreword

For many years I have enjoyed a good relationship with the Council for Christian Colleges & Universities. The last three presidents have been personal friends and I have spoken on dozens of CCCU campuses during my years as Governor and U.S. Senator.

On different occasions, the association leaders graciously invited me to speak at some of their meetings, to serve on the board of reference and the board of directors, and to cochair a capital campaign. I have observed the Council's growth with keen interest and admiration.

I am delighted that the CCCU story is now being made available in book form. Professor Patterson provides us with a better understanding of how the Council came into being, and then narrates the many personalities, programs, and other activities that have been a part of CCCU history for the last twenty-five years. On the occasion of this silver anniversary, I commend the reading of this volume to all who identify with the cause of distinctly Christian higher education.

Hon. Mark O. Hatfield
Former U.S. Senator (Oregon)

Preface

Much of the recent literature regarding Christian higher education in the United States paints a rather dismal picture of the steady, long-term secularization that has eroded the religious identities of once proudly Christian institutions.[1] In perhaps the most provocative study of this issue to date, James Burtchaell's *The Dying of the Light* features seventeen American colleges and universities from a wide range of denominational backgrounds, all of which are judged to have distanced themselves in significant ways from their original sponsoring churches. In fact, this Roman Catholic cleric and scholar submits that his case studies invite reflection on "the dynamics whereby any Christian endeavor can unwittingly be decomposed."[2] Burtchaell does not even find many encouraging glimmers in the two evangelical schools that he investigates, Azusa Pacific University and Dordt College, both members of the Council for Christian Colleges & Universities.[3] His tome conveys the unmistakable impression that Christian higher education at the turn of the century faces a precarious future.

While Burtchaell's diagnosis certainly contains appropriate warnings about academic institutions surrendering their Christian distinctives, it offers a limited, almost begrudging recognition of schools that have refused to extinguish the "light" of genuine faith. Indeed, the twenty-five-year history of the CCCU reveals that its membership has consistently carried the torch for Christ-centered higher education. The continuing vitality of the Christian college movement suggests that the imagery of Burtchaell's title, while applicable to the nominally

Christian sector of academe, fails to typify institutions that are actively engaged in the integration of faith, scholarship, and service.

The story told here focuses primarily on the unique philosophy, programs, and personalities that have shaped the CCCU. At the same time, the broader contexts that inform the CCCU's relatively short institutional history cannot be ignored. The rich heritage of Christian higher education in America dating back to the seventeenth century formed an important backdrop to the 1976 founding of what was then called the Christian College Coalition.[4] Another crucial development for the Christian college enterprise was the remarkable resurgence of American evangelicalism as it distanced itself from fundamentalism during the post–World War II era; conservative Protestantism's renewed vision of cultural engagement and cooperative endeavor held special relevance for its institutions of higher learning. Finally, the roles of the Christian College Consortium, first as a parent body and later as a sister organization, represent an indispensable segment of the CCCU story.

I wish to thank all those who supplied information, granted interviews, or in other ways made my research and writing tasks easier. In particular, I wish to express sincere gratitude to Bob Andringa and the CCCU staff for their tremendous support throughout the process, including a week-long visit to the Washington headquarters in January of 2000. My stay there was memorable not only for an unexpected fire that broke out in an apartment housing students in the American Studies Program, but also for the opportunity to be the first occupant of a newly-renovated guest apartment in the townhouse across the alley from The Dellenback Center. CCCU staff who provided special assistance include Marge Bernbaum, Rich Gathro, Jerry Herbert, Jennifer Jukanovich, Julie Peterson, Richard Potts, Kisha Ross, and Lauren Sable. The Washington trip also allowed me to attend the CCCU's annual meeting for presidents of member institutions and to interview many individuals who have been part of CCCU history.

Several other people proved to be invaluable contributors to this volume. John Dellenback, former CCCU president, and his wife Mary Jane generously underwrote most of the project expenses through their Agape Foundation. Tom Englund, president of the Christian College Consortium, sent copies of pertinent Consortium minutes, allowed me to borrow a dissertation on the Consortium, and met with my wife and me for an interview in Concord, New Hampshire. Karen Longman, former CCCU vice president for professional development and research, and now the chief academic officer at Greenville College in Illinois, graciously consented to an interview on her campus and also gave me copies of several important materials from her files. As the documentation indicates, many others worked telephone interviews into their busy schedules.

Since the bulk of my research and writing was done during my first year as a faculty member at Union University, I am deeply indebted to the school's administration for its tangible support and encouragement. President David Dockery recommended me to Bob Andringa as a possible author, arranged for a Union financial donation to the project, authorized a reduced teaching load, gave an interview on CCCU conferences for new presidents, and advised on the title of the book. Provost Carla Sanderson, arts and sciences dean Barbara McMillin, and Christian Studies chair George Guthrie worked out the logistics of my released time from the classroom; in addition, during my interview with Dr. Sanderson, she shared about her experiences in CCCU leadership institutes. Information services librarian Melissa Moore expeditiously arranged for some interlibrary loan material.

On other fronts, Calvin College invited me to participate in a 1999 summer seminar on American evangelicalism and fundamentalism, which was led by George Marsden of Notre Dame University. This provided me with opportunities to think about some of the larger contexts related to CCCU history and to conduct some initial interviews. At home, my wife Donna and son David remained patient and sympathetic, even when I tied up the family computer for long stretches of time. My daughter and son-in-law, Becky and Brent Lollar, lent interest and moral support. Finally, Baker Books and editor Robert Hosack worked conscientiously to keep the manuscript on a fast track for publication.

Soli Deo Gloria

J. A. P.
Jackson, Tennessee
September 2000

ONE

The Past Is Prologue: Protestant Higher Education in America

The Idea of a Christian University

The membership of the Council for Christian Colleges & Universities reflects significant curricular, financial, geographical, denominational, and theological diversity. Nevertheless, the CCCU's constituents enthusiastically embrace a shared vision for the purposes and priorities of Christian higher education. D. A. Carson, Research Professor of New Testament at Trinity International University, catches the spirit of that vision in several of his theses about the distinctive attributes of a Christian university: (1) it is God-centered and loyal to the Christian revelation, particularly as focused on Jesus Christ and his gospel; (2) it commits itself to the formation and maintenance of a Christian worldview; (3) it is marked by humility of mind and a communal care that fosters integrity and candor; (4) it is beholden to the church, the world, and God; (5) it grapples with issues of Christianity and culture; and (6) it seeks to balance academic freedom and confessional fidelity.[1] While Carson was not officially writing for the CCCU, his philosophy meshes well with what that organization has been articulating for twenty-five years. Moreover, Carson's propositions offer a useful tool for assessing the historical development of the Christian academy.

The earliest roots of Christian educational endeavor ultimately track to the Old Testament, particularly in the admonitions that parents pass on to their children the truths about God (Deut. 6), as well as in the didactic roles of the prophets and scribes. Although drawing on Jewish pedagogy, the teaching ministries of Jesus and the apostolic church helped to establish a discretely Christian instructional approach. By the late second century, ventures like the catechetical school in Alexandria, Egypt, creatively blended Christian doctrine with classical influences from the Greek philosophical academies. Toward the end of the patristic age, Augustine of Hippo argued for the usefulness of the traditional liberal arts (grammar, dialectic, rhetoric, arithmetic, geometry, music, and astronomy) in the interpretation and proclamation of Scripture.[2]

During the early Middle Ages, the Augustinian synthesis inspired the founding of monastic and cathedral schools in many parts of Western Europe, meeting both cultural and ecclesiastical needs. These educational auxiliaries of the Roman Catholic Church, along with the self-governing guilds of masters and students that appeared later, set the stage for the birth of universities in the late twelfth and early thirteenth centuries. Carson delineates the essentially Christian character of these medieval institutions:

> Western universities began with a strong emphasis on the unity of knowledge, on the university. What held it together was the notion of revelation, and broad consensus that there is one Mind, the mind of the personal-transcendent God, that unites all knowledge and truth in himself.[3]

Thus the medieval universities consciously promoted the integration of faith and learning by recognizing a reference point from which to evaluate the ideas of "pagan" thinkers like Aristotle. They accordingly accepted the principle that "all truth is God's truth." This developing concept of the Christian university remained intact during the Reformation, even though Protestant educators—and some Catholic reformers—implemented curricular changes that reflected the growing impact of Christian humanism.[4]

Colonial American Colleges

New England Puritans first launched the Christian higher education enterprise in North America with the founding of Harvard College in 1636. As George Marsden explains, Harvard was fundamentally an English Reformation school modeled after Emmanuel College of the University of Cambridge.[5] Indeed, Puritans on both sides of the Atlantic shared the Reformation ideal that education should entail "a comprehensive study of human knowledge in all its branches within a context of biblical revelation."[6] Thus Harvard not only stood in continuity with past expressions of the Christian academy; the Massachusetts Bay institution also anticipated other collegiate experiments that in due time would unfold in the American colonies.

Very early in its history, Harvard committed itself to be a Christ-centered college, pledging to instruct and persuade every student to consider that the primary purpose of life and study "is to know God and Jesus Christ which is eternal life, Joh. 17:3, and therefore to lay Christ in the bottom, as the only foundation of all sound knowledge and learning."[7] Harvard, of course, struggled to sustain that noble aim; by the early eighteenth century, disgruntled Puritans, including Increase and Cotton Mather of Boston, sensed a decline in Calvinist orthodoxy at Harvard. Hence, Congregationalist clergy in Connecticut established Yale College in 1701 as a theologically safer alternative. For its part, Harvard assumed a decidedly Arminian posture, which prevailed until the school's eventual drift toward Unitarianism by the early nineteenth century.[8]

Most other colonial colleges, like Harvard and Yale, began as resolutely Christian undertakings, and often were affiliated with specific Protestant denominations. In several cases, the First Great Awakening proved to be a primary catalyst for educational advance as New Light clergy sought to conserve the spiritual fruits of the revival by training a new generation of ministers. The Presbyterians founded Princeton (1746), the Baptists founded Brown (1764), the Dutch Reformed founded Rutgers (1766), and the Congregationalists founded Dartmouth (1769).[9]

Early American institutions of higher learning, however, were not seminaries or Bible colleges. In their cultural context, they accepted the responsibility for training the elite of colonial society, some of whom were not professing Christians and many of whom did not aspire to be preachers. Following the model of early Harvard, the curricula of these schools incorporated biblical and theological studies with traditional liberal arts, including "pagan" learning.[10] While this suggests a closer affinity with the philosophy of the CCCU, the colonial colleges cooperated with government in ways that would not be possible for modern Christian institutions. The public/private distinction simply did not exist in colonial America; the schools acknowledged some public duties and frequently welcomed direct state subsidies to help stay afloat financially.[11]

Colonial collegiate education eloquently testifies to what William Ringenberg of Taylor University calls a "pervading Christian purpose."[12] A sizable majority of colonial colleges conscientiously pursued a palpable mission for Christ and his kingdom. Certainly Christian higher education in America began to build a significant legacy in the formative years leading up to the American Revolution.

From the Revolution to the Civil War

Educational patterns from American independence through the antebellum years manifested substantial continuity with those of the colonial epoch. During this time, a Protestant quasi-establishment effectively dominated religious and cultural life in America, so it is not surprising that higher education retained its conspicuously Christian orientation. Both Christian beliefs and moral principles held sway not only in the oldest colleges, but also in the scores of newly-founded schools.

The first half of the nineteenth century witnessed a booming growth of collegiate institutions in the United States, with Presbyterians, Methodists, Baptists, and Congregationalists leading the way in sponsoring these new efforts. Just as in the colonial era, revival once again sparked educational expansion. The Second Great Awakening brought times of spiritual renewal to the established colleges like Yale and Princeton; it also helped to generate a new missionary impulse, some of which was channeled into planting schools in the frontier areas of the Midwest and South. Institutions like Union University (1823), Taylor University (1846), and Wheaton College (1860), all currently members of the CCCU, trace their origins to a period when there existed a dynamic link between education and evangelical revivalism.[13]

Another important development that marked the years of the early republic was the attempt of Christian educators to come to terms with the Enlightenment, the scientific and philosophical revolution that had been birthed in Europe. Led by college presidents like John Wither-spoon of Princeton and Timothy Dwight of Yale, this ambitious project called for a creative synthesis of faith and reason. As Wheaton professor Mark Noll has said, many American intellectuals drew inspiration from the more conservative "didactic" Enlightenment that was most fittingly expressed in Scottish Common Sense Realism.[14] This framework allowed evangelical academicians to work hard at integrating Christian faith with the empirical science of Francis Bacon, John Locke, and Isaac Newton. It also helped to shape the senior-year moral philosophy course, which blossomed at many American colleges in the nineteenth century. Usually taught by school presidents, this pivotal piece of the curriculum encompassed apologetics, epistemology, ethics, citizenship, and a number of other topics.[15]

These experiments in the integration of faith and learning departed somewhat from the older Puritan model. As Noll explains, the shift raised some foundational questions concerning the goals of Christian higher education:

> Puritans had grounded their thinking in special revelation and had worked to turn special revelation into a framework for all of learning. The educators of the new United States, however, grounded their thinking in the Enlightenment and worked to give special revelation a place within that framework.[16]

While this change may appear to be subtle, it suggested that Christian intellectuals had allied themselves too closely with some features of Enlightenment ideology. This would have enormous implications when the "academic revolution" hit full force in the post–Civil War period.[17]

Secularization and Responses

In the decades that followed the Civil War, American society underwent a transformation of monumental proportions. Rapid industrialization and urbanization forever changed the socio-economic life of the nation. New surges in immigration brought larger numbers of Roman Catholics, Jews, and Eastern Orthodox to the United States; a growing pluralism thereby undermined the Protestant cultural hegemony that had prevailed for so long. On the theological front, Darwinian evolution and a higher critical approach to the Bible created the climate for the flowering of Protestant liberalism, while intensified concerns about cities and the new industrial order stimulated the rise of the social gospel. At the same time, revivalism seemed to have lost some of its potency as an agent of cultural reformation.[18] All of these trends served to challenge the world of Christian higher education.

Between the Civil War and the Great Depression, the American university came of age. State institutions, which previously embodied a nonsectarian Protestant ethos, moved increasingly further away from any overt expression of religious allegiance. Some older elite colleges that were founded on a Christian base achieved university status and gradually shed most of their evangelical Christian distinctives; although the pace of these changes varied from school to school, secularization proved irreversible. New elite universities like Cornell, Stanford, and Johns Hopkins emerged with funding from industrial barons, but with little if any recognition of Christian educational principles. Finally, many of the church-related institutions that had been established in the antebellum period began what was an often protracted process of muting both their Christian and denominational commitments. The overall scene, as historian Noll depicts, was unmistakable: "In almost every way imaginable the new university undercut the traditional values of Christian higher education in America."[19]

What was behind this dramatic secularization of American universities during the late nineteenth and early twentieth centuries? Certainly part of the explanation can be found in several structural changes that appeared at many institutions of higher learning: wealth from the new economic order changed educational funding patterns; the German university model of specialized scholarship made substantial inroads; curricula consequently expanded, especially with the growth of professional and graduate programs; and, with the Morrill Act of 1862 and the Hatch Act of 1887, the federal government initiated a limited involvement in higher education.[20]

Perhaps a more important reason for academic secularization was the declining appeal of a Christian worldview as the integrative center of educational pursuits. As both Noll and Marsden have demonstrated, moral philosophy in general and Scottish Common Sense Realism in particular lost an intellectual battle to scientific naturalism and philosophical pragmatism. Christian educators failed to develop a new model for the integration of faith and learning that would transcend the limitations of the older Enlightenment-based approach.

Moreover, it became increasingly difficult to connect Christian doctrine to the various academic disciplines because the theological seminaries had been set up largely as separate institutions from the colleges and universities.[21]

Marsden also points to the irony of liberal Protestantism's adjustments to social and intellectual change. Liberals, clearly uncomfortable with many aspects of traditional orthodoxy, preferred to emphasize the moral rather than the doctrinal dimensions of the Christian faith. They fervently hoped to mold the environment of the modern university with a nonsectarian, basically naturalistic ideology that valued freedom, theological tolerance, and service to humanity. In the long run, as Marsden perceptively asserts, their project collapsed on them:

> The logic of nonsectarian ideals which the Protestant establishment had successfully promoted in public life dictated that liberal Protestantism itself should be moved to the periphery to which other religious perspectives had been relegated for some time. The result was an "inclusive" higher education that resolved the problems of pluralism by virtually excluding all religious perspectives from the nation's highest academic life.[22]

Thus, liberal Protestant educational leaders, perhaps unwittingly, promoted secularization. While they cannot be blamed for what happened at universities lacking a Christian foundation, they are culpable on some level. By uncritically acclimating themselves to the spirit of the age, they allowed many of their own schools to fall victim to what D. A. Carson calls "a universal tendency for Christian universities to drift toward the dominant voices in the culture, especially the dominant intellectual voices in the culture."[23]

Despite the tumultuous changes wrought by the academic revolution, some institutions successfully managed to maintain the Christian heritage in higher education. For example, the historic African American colleges, most of which were organized after the Civil War, continued to foster Christian educational and missionary agendas.[24] Another notable response to the secularization of the academy can be found in the Bible college movement launched in the 1880s. Partly in reaction to what was happening in university and seminary settings, Bible institutes and colleges established Bible-based curricula emphasizing practical training for ministry. By the 1920s, many of these schools became identified with fundamentalism, which by then was battling modernism in the mainline Protestant denominations. Since then, Bible colleges have continued to represent a major force within conservative evangelicalism. Some of the schools affiliated with the CCCU that began as Bible colleges include Biola University, Gordon College, Malone College, Nyack College, and Simpson College.[25]

Some of the "old-time" colleges founded before the Civil War also resisted secularization. For example, Wheaton College in Illinois sustained its evangelical convictions, even as schools with similar backgrounds succumbed to liberal or secular influences. Like some of the Bible colleges, Wheaton acquired a reputation in the 1920s and 1930s as a fundamentalist institution, a label frequently applied to any Protestant schools that stood against the academic flow of that era.[26]

In reality, ascertaining the relationship of Christian colleges to fundamentalism can be tricky. Since some evangelicals today share Mark Noll's judgment that fundamentalism was an "intellectual disaster," their attitudes toward the historic movement are at best ambivalent.[27] Nevertheless, some current CCCU members, such as Taylor (1846), Geneva (1848), and Houghton (1883), were widely perceived as fundamentalist schools in the 1920s, even though they were all founded well before fundamentalism surfaced as a distinct movement. However, some CCCU institutions were started as more explicitly fundamentalist projects, namely Bryan (1930) and Westmont (1937). The picture gets fuzzier for CCCU members that were founded during the academic revolution by smaller, conservative denominations, some of which retained a strong ethnic identity. Colleges like Calvin (Christian Reformed [1876]), North Park (Evangelical Covenant [1891]), Eastern Nazarene (Nazarene [1900]), Goshen (Mennonite [1902]), Messiah (Brethren in Christ [1909]), and Lee (Church of God, Cleveland, Tennessee [1918]) all displayed much more ambiguous connections with fundamentalism.[28] At the same time, the historian dare not overlook fundamentalism's hostility toward secularization nor the role it played in sheltering Christian higher education in a time of crisis.

The Post–World War II Evangelical Resurgence

As Joel Carpenter's masterful *Revive Us Again* demonstrates, fundamentalism's apparent cultural disengagement after the Scopes Trial of 1925 actually veiled the movement's energetic efforts in the 1930s and

1940s to build an extensive network of schools, mission agencies, youth organizations, publications, and broadcasting ventures. Fundamentalist legwork paid off, setting the stage for the remarkable emergence of a new evangelical coalition following World War II. In light of this, Carpenter ranks fundamentalism as "probably the most broadly influential American evangelical movement in the second third of the twentieth century," noting that "its ideas, outlook, and religious 'goods and services' penetrated virtually all of the other movements and traditions."[29]

The new evangelicalism of the post–World War II era vigorously challenged conservative Protestants to rethink some of their cherished assumptions. Without slighting traditional priorities like personal piety and evangelism, post-war evangelical leaders called for fundamentalists to move beyond their cultural isolationism and ecclesiastical separatism. Theologian Carl F. H. Henry, a forceful advocate of Christian higher education, faulted older fundamentalism for its failure to set forth a biblical worldview and for its woefully deficient social ethic.[30] Boston pastor Harold J. Ockenga, who later served as president of Gordon College, and revivalist Billy Graham, a Wheaton College graduate, steadfastly urged conservative evangelicals to put aside their minor differences and to support cooperative endeavors in evangelism, publishing, and education.[31] As these leaders helped to build a movement, they inevitably addressed some issues that were relevant to Christian higher education. Further, they realized that Christian schools potentially could offer intellectual and professional resources for the support of evangelicalism.

During the 1930s and 1940s, however, most conservative Protestant colleges were in a survival mode. Still licking their wounds from the fundamentalist-modernist controversy, they coped valiantly with meager financial resources during the Great Depression and World War II. As secularization continued at many mainline denominational colleges and universities, more conservative schools functioned, in the words of Gordon College professor Thomas Askew, as "insular, church-focused" institutions.[32] With the exception of schools like Wheaton and Calvin, high academic standards often were conspicuously absent. At many Christian colleges, faculty members worked long hours for low salaries, and some lacked full teaching credentials. Classroom instruction, according to Askew, "tended to be largely descriptive rather than analytical and exploratory."[33] Moreover, it seems that few professors enjoyed time for serious scholarship or professional development.

After World War II, evangelical higher education entered what William Ringenberg has termed a "reconstruction" phase or "recovery process."[34] Several factors help to explain the growing strength of Christian colleges in the post-war period: (1) the evangelical resurgence energized the movement's educational institutions, making them more visible, confident, and culturally engaged; (2) general economic prosperity and government programs like the GI Bill allowed more young people to attend college; (3) an increase of jobs requiring postsecondary education further aided enrollments; (4) a growing awareness of distinctly Christian higher education made it more attractive to evangelical parents; and (5) overall, Christian institutions worked hard to improve the quality of what they offered.[35] Obviously, some of these explanations apply to American higher education in general; Christian schools benefited from some of the same things that boosted secular institutions in the boom years following World War II. At the same time, conservative Protestant colleges clearly gained stature by emphasizing some of their singular features.

In the 1950s and 1960s, Christian schools expended considerable effort on matters of definition, credentialing, and consolidation.[36] In the process of defining themselves, evangelical institutions drew on both theology and history. First, they picked up on Carl Henry's challenge to cultivate distinctly Christian perspectives on learning. Second, as Askew observes, they tacitly affirmed that the past is prologue:

> In securing the confidence of the evangelical public, the conservative Christian colleges also recaptured a historical legitimacy, claiming origins in the colonial and nineteenth-century colleges, and ultimately reaching back to Geneva, Cambridge, Oxford, and the medieval heritage of Christian learning. In doing so these campuses sought an identity, not as something novel on the educational scene, but as inheritors of a long, noble tradition.[37]

As the evangelical educational enterprise developed a keener sense of its historical roots, it consequently matured in terms of its unique identity and mission.

Christian colleges also enhanced their institutional credentials throughout the 1950s and 1960s. Several important matters relating to academic standards received more serious attention at many conservative evangelical campuses: faculty salaries; professorial qualifications, including a stronger emphasis on terminal degrees; regional accreditation; and specialized accreditation through agencies like the National Council for the Accreditation of Teacher Education and the National Association of Schools of Music.[38] While not all Christian schools improved at the same pace and low self-esteem sometimes lingered, the overall progress of evangelical higher education was encouraging.

In terms of consolidation, some of this was internal as individual schools refined their goals and curricula based on their own "traditions, obligations, ideals, and momentum."[39] On the external level, the creation of the Council for the Advancement of Small Colleges (CASC) in 1955 (now the Council of Independent Colleges) proved to be advantageous for the Christian institutions that joined. First, the Council assisted small schools in gaining accreditation and federal funding. Second, for newly-founded Christian institutions like LeTourneau (1946), Bethel in Indiana (1947), Oklahoma Christian (1950), Eastern (1952), Judson (1963), and Oral Roberts (1963), CASC offered workshops and other helpful resources. Third, a pattern for Christian college involvement in educational associations was firmly established. Previously, cooperative ventures among Christian schools had been limited to denominational fellowships like those in the Southern Baptist Convention or the Church of the Nazarene. As Thomas Askew elucidates, participation in CASC allowed conservative Protestant colleges to develop "lasting institutional and personal linkages . . . across theological, denominational, and geographic boundaries."[40] When the time came to organize educational associations for evangelical schools, those already existing "linkages" would confirm their worth.

Through the mid-1960s, a relatively small but recognizable group of conservative evangelical colleges continued to hold the banner for genuinely Christian higher education. Unlike most mainline Protestant schools, they stood firmly against the tides of secularization that had transformed so much in American postsecondary education for several decades. In the process of sustaining the principles that have set Christian institutions apart, these colleges gained a deeper appreciation for the historic legacy of which they were beneficiaries. In addition, they reached a point where they understood both the need for and value of greater collaboration among themselves.

TWO

A Parent Organization: The Christian College Consortium

Background

By the late 1950s some evangelical educators and other leaders began exploring various options for cooperative academic endeavors. During his New York City crusade in 1957, for example, Billy Graham met with a small group to discuss the possibility of creating a Christian university. The following year David McKenna, then vice president at Spring Arbor College in Michigan, proposed that Free Methodist schools work together in more meaningful ways.[1] Graham's role in evangelical higher education, even when the Christian university idea was debated in earnest during the 1960s, would remain more circumscribed because of the demands of his revivalistic ministry. On the other hand, McKenna later emerged as a key figure in the promotion of collaborative efforts by evangelical colleges.

During the 1960s *Christianity Today* editor Carl Henry used his magazine to advocate new initiatives for evangelical higher education. As early as 1962 he editorialized in favor of a "federated campus" at Gordon College in Massachusetts as a way of consolidating Christian collegiate education in the Northeast. Henry preferred the notion of a Christian university, but commented that the federated plan "might emerge more naturally by evangelical cooperation from the bottom up."[2] The next year, the journalist-theologian offered several additional suggestions for strengthening the evangelical educational enterprise, including: the development of specialties at each accredited Christian college; cooperative summer institutes at the graduate level; a rotating faculty drawn from "leading evangelical colleges"; and "an international, interdenominational Christian university," which he labeled "imperative."[3]

In the meantime, conservative Protestant colleges received a bit of a jolt in 1965 when they discovered that the soon-to-be-released Danforth Foundation report on 817 church-related colleges contained a classification scheme that was not especially conducive to their cause. The report confirmed evangelical suspicions about the secularizing trends at many mainline denominational schools; but it also utilized the implicitly derogatory term "defender of the faith college" to describe most conservative institutions. In Washington, Henry met with several evangelical college presidents, and they proposed "faith-affirming" as a more suitable designation for schools that did not wish to be identified as fundamentalist. The published version of the Danforth report left the original taxonomy intact, but duly acknowledged the "faith-affirming" recommendation in a footnote.[4] The whole episode served to reinforce the need for evangelical schools to work together to protect their interests.

By 1966 Henry's vision for a Christian university received new impetus. At the annual meeting of the National Association of Evangelicals (NAE), Wheaton president Hudson Armerding sketched a plan for an evangelical university to be "composed of cooperating regionally accredited Christian liberal arts colleges."[5] His suggestion went well beyond the proposal for an association of evangelical colleges that was made by the NAE's Commission on Higher Education.[6]

By this time, Henry had settled on the New York City area as a feasible location for a Christian university, estimating that $75 million dollars would be needed to start the project.[7] At a two-day evangelical conference on higher education held at Indiana University in September of 1966, Henry again set forth his dream of a university to "train young intellectuals to introduce Christian ideas and ideals into all areas of dialogue, reflection, and work." At the same time, he seemed to sense that evangelicalism might not be ready for such an undertaking, so he proffered the concept of an "Institute for Advanced Christian Studies" as an "ideal intermediate venture."[8]

Participants at the Indiana meeting, which was funded by the Lilly Endowment and the Indiana University Foundation, also examined other possible initiatives. John Snyder, then an administrator at Indiana, favored the establishment of satellite Christian colleges at public university campuses. David McKenna presented a consortium model, which was popular in higher education circles in the 1960s, as the most workable for bringing evangelical colleges together. McKenna also profiled a plan for an "Academy of Christian Scholars," which seemed to have some affinity with Henry's idea. The Indiana consultation additionally broached the plausibility of Christian colleges developing cooperative graduate programs.[9]

The conference at Indiana University represented a major advance for evangelicals who were seeking to achieve greater coordination in their higher educational enterprise. First, speakers placed several tangible options on the table for future dialogue and planning; for example, later in 1966 evangelical leaders discussed the university idea at a session held in conjunction with the Berlin Congress on World Evangelism.[10] Second, the Indiana meeting led directly to the formation of the Institute for Advanced Christian Studies (IFACS) as a vehicle to promote evangelical scholarship across the academic disciplines. Under the leadership of Snyder and Henry, IFACS obtained funding from the Lilly Endowment and used it to sponsor several writing projects. Subsequently, Lilly grants also allowed IFACS to serve as a catalyst in fulfilling McKenna's hopes for a consortium of Christian schools.[11]

Further developments after the Indiana consultation highlighted the fact that a new era in the history of evangelical higher education was unfolding, one that Thomas Askew designates with the heading "professionalization, networks, and theoretical understanding."[12] Evidence of networking by evangelicals in academe, in fact, continued to accumulate. For example, learned societies like the Conference on Faith and History (1967) began to be organized in the late 1960s and early 1970s, bringing together Christian professors in their teaching disciplines.[13] Then in 1970 the *Gordon Review* became the *Christian Scholar's Review*, involving faculty from several Christian institutions in a unique publishing venture.[14] Finally, evangelical college presidents set the stage for more formal cooperation in the fellowship and interaction that they enjoyed at meetings of the Association of American Colleges and the American Association of Presidents of Independent Colleges and Universities.[15]

The Tempe Conference and the Launch of the Christian College Consortium

In the late 1960s a perceived crisis in evangelical higher education stimulated further conversations among its advocates. David McKenna, who left Spring Arbor to assume the presidency of Seattle Pacific in 1968, and John Snyder, who became Westmont's fourth president in 1969, continued to prod other evangelical educators about the urgency of augmenting their cooperative efforts given the financial, enrollment, and identity issues facing Christian colleges. They helped to arrange meetings in Chicago with a small number of institutional presidents in both 1969 and 1970. At the second caucus, McKenna, Snyder, Armerding, and Robert Sandin, a professor at the University of Toledo, reached a decision to approach IFACS concerning financial support for a conference to be held late in 1970. IFACS granted the funding request and assigned Donald Youngren, its executive secretary, the task of working with college presidents to set up a meeting in Tempe, Arizona. Sandin, a sympathetic observer of evangelical higher education, played a key role in setting the agenda and suggesting speakers. He also agreed to serve as recording secretary for the conference.[16]

In December of 1970 the presidents of eleven evangelical colleges gathered in Tempe to hear papers and discuss the future of their movement. The list of participating executives included the following: Hudson Armerding (Wheaton), Myron Augsburger (Eastern Mennonite), James Baird (Oklahoma Christian), Everett Cattell (Malone), Ray Hostetter (Messiah), Dennis Kinlaw (Asbury), Carl Lundquist (Bethel of Minnesota), David McKenna (Seattle Pacific), Harold Ockenga (Gordon), Milo Rediger (Taylor), and John Snyder (Westmont).[17] Several in this group, most notably Armerding, Kinlaw, Lundquist, McKenna, and Snyder, ensured some continuity with the earlier Indiana and Chicago meetings.

Three major papers were delivered to the presidents in Tempe. Earl McGrath, the director of the Higher Education Center at Temple University in Philadelphia, explicitly put forth the idea of a consortium of Christian colleges as the type of project that would allow member schools to "attract the financial, professional, and social support necessary for survival as effective centers of learning."[18] William Jellema, the executive associate and research director for the Association of American Colleges, endorsed the consortium proposal; he also challenged the participants to develop a distinctive rationale, such as the integration of faith and learning, for Christian higher education.[19] Carl Henry offered a third perspective, emphasizing the evangelistic and apologetic responsibilities of the faith-affirming colleges represented at Tempe. He characteristically urged them to propel "a systematic theistic view into a naturalistic climate" and to delineate "the unified view of life required by revelational theism."[20] While Henry did not directly speak to the consortium idea, several months later he indicated that this type of evangelical cooperation was preferable to "the ghetto-survival of a small and diminishing number of isolated institutions."[21]

The Tempe consultation eminently succeeded in building a consensus for a consortium of evangelical colleges. At the same time, the presidents kept alive Henry's hope for a Christian university, at least as a long-range goal. While the concept of a university system was not a central theme in any of the papers, the minutes reveal that it occupied a significant part of the discussion time.[22]

The achievements of the Tempe conference became clearer in the follow-up planning that began in early 1971. In January several presidents dialogued further during the Association of American Colleges meetings in Cincinnati. Nine of the eleven schools that were represented in Tempe stood prepared to help fund a consortium. In addition, IFACS pledged $22,000 to assist with the consortium's first-year budget. Robert Sandin, a key facilitator at Tempe, advised that the cooperating schools establish a commission to begin exploring the appropriate structure for an evangelical university.[23] Although some of the logistics still had to be worked out, most of the necessary ingredients were in place for the new consortium.

In March 1971, presidents of prospective member colleges gathered in Chicago, where they voted to proceed with the incorporation of the Christian College Consortium. The fledgling organization held its first official meeting in May 1971, also in Chicago. The first executive committee consisted of David McKenna (chairman), Carl Lundquist (vice-chairman), Milo Rediger (secretary/treasurer), and Hudson Armerding and Ray Hostetter (members-at-large).[24]

One of the most important documents in the early history of the Christian College Consortium was its Statement of Purposes, which was filed with the Articles of Incorporation in July 1971. The Statement proposed an ambitious agenda, one that encompassed many of the themes that had been considered from the Indiana consultation in 1966 to the Tempe meeting in 1970:

> To promote the purposes of evangelical Christian higher education in the church and in society through the promotion of cooperation among evangelical colleges, and, in that conviction, to encourage and support scholarly research among Christian scholars for the purpose of integrating faith and learning; to initiate programs to improve the quality of instructional programs and encourage innovation in member institutions; to conduct research into the effectiveness of the educational programs of the member colleges, with particular emphasis upon student development; to improve the management efficiency of the member institutions; to expand the human, financial and material resources available to the member institutions; to explore the feasibility of a university system of Christian colleges; and to do and perform all and everything which may be necessary and proper for the conduct of the activities of this organization in furtherance of the purposes heretofore expressed.[25]

Thus the Consortium positioned itself to play a unique and strategic role in Christian higher education. While it ultimately fell short in accomplishing some of its goals, its very existence attested to a commendable vitality and maturity in the evangelical academy.

Membership

The ten charter members of the Christian College Consortium included Bethel of Minnesota, Eastern Mennonite, Gordon, Greenville, Malone, Messiah, Seattle Pacific, Taylor, Westmont, and Wheaton.[26] The primary criteria that guided the initial membership invitations called for each school to demonstrate sufficient economic resources, a commitment to the integration of faith and learning, the stature of the institution's president in Christian higher education, and a location that would aid the Consortium in attaining a regional mix.[27] Although denominational affiliations apparently were not an explicit consideration for membership, the Consortium nonetheless reflected a noteworthy balance for a small organization. Four of the colleges were independent or nondenominational (Gordon, Taylor, Westmont, and Wheaton). The other six represented five different denominational traditions: Baptist General Conference (Bethel), Mennonite (Eastern Mennonite), Free Methodist (Greenville and Seattle Pacific), Evangelical Friends (Malone), and Brethren in Christ (Messiah). Hence, the Consortium membership exemplified what the late historian Timothy Smith referred to as the "evangelical kaleidoscope."[28] In other words, the Consortium embodied the diversity and pluralism of the entire evangelical movement, particularly as it had unfolded since World War II. By embracing the richness and breadth of evangelicalism, the "faith-affirming" colleges of the Consortium clearly intended to distance the organization from fundamentalism. Indeed, a statement of faith from the National Association of Evangelicals functioned as the doctrinal standard for the Consortium.[29]

Membership in the Consortium remained fairly stable over the years. The four additions to the original ten further enhanced the denominational diversity: George Fox (Evangelical Friends) and Houghton (Wesleyan) were admitted in 1973; Trinity (Evangelical Free) and Asbury (independent) joined in 1976. The only institution to leave was Eastern Mennonite, which cited a financial concern about membership fees when it withdrew in 1978.[30] Even though some minor expansion in membership was debated, the Consortium resolved by the mid-1970s to stay small; this decision, of course, helped to precipitate the establishment of a parallel association, now known as the CCCU.

The Integration of Faith and Learning

In July of 1971 Edward Neteland left his position as president of a learning resources company in Chicago to become the first executive director of the Christian College Consortium. He also brought to this new position prior experience in Christian higher education as an administrator at Trinity College in Deerfield, Illinois. Since he was already rooted in the Chicago area, he ran the Consortium from an office near the O'Hare Airport. Neteland primarily focused his energies on trying to develop a university system of Christian colleges, which was one of the Consortium's announced goals. Unfortunately, as former Gordon College president Richard Gross once remarked, "none of the Consortium institutions had university-type resources."[31] Neteland resigned his leadership position in March of 1973, at which time David McKenna agreed to serve as interim executive director and move the Consortium headquarters to Seattle.[32] By 1976 the Consortium dropped the university concept from its stated objectives.[33]

As the dream of a Christian university gradually receded in importance, it is not surprising that the integration of faith and learning rose to the forefront as a crucial Consortium priority. To some degree, the transition from Neteland to McKenna underlined a shift of emphasis that had already been brewing. In fact, McKenna authored a programmatic piece on the integration principle for a Consortium publication in 1972.[34] At about the same time, the Seattle Pacific president drafted a grant proposal to the Lilly Endowment that sought financial backing for integration programs and other Consortium initiatives. Lilly then awarded the Consortium its first external funding— $300,000—in 1973.[35]

The Consortium had actually sponsored its first faith and learning workshop for faculty several months before the Lilly money was made available. In August of 1972 an institute was held in Chicago at North Park College, which was not a Consortium school. Workshop leaders included Calvin College philosopher Nicholas Wolterstorff, historian J. Edwin Orr, and Stuart Barton Babbage, an Australian evangelical known for bringing Christian perspectives to bear on culture. These institutes, renamed the Faith/Learning/Living Seminars in 1974, explored not only issues related to integration, but also the historical, educational, biblical, and philosophical foundations of the Christian liberal arts college.[36] They became the prototype for similar workshops developed in the 1980s by the Christian College Coalition.

While the Consortium certainly contributed to a wider understanding of how to integrate faith and learning at member institutions, it did not invent the concept. As the previous chapter indicates, the principle that faith demands a distinctive approach to learning has been an essential part of Christian higher education for a long time. In the context of the evangelical academy since World War II, however, it appears that the integration impulse can be traced to three important and related sources.

First, the Consortium emphasis on integration derives in part from what might be called the "Carl Henry Project." Henry hammered away for years on the need for Christians to think in terms of worldviews and to challenge prevailing cultural assumptions. In many ways, he based his vision for both IFACS and a Christian university on an integration model. Henry may have done little teaching in Christian colleges, but he exercised considerable influence on the thinking of those who did. His speaking role at the Tempe conference in 1970 simply confirmed his significance for both evangelicalism and its educational enterprise.[37]

Second, a faith and learning program for faculty that Wheaton College started in the late 1960s provided a useful exemplar for Consortium leaders to consider. Frank Gaebelein, former headmaster at the Stony Brook School and a onetime colleague of Henry at *Christianity Today*, directed the first faculty workshop in 1969.[38] Eventually, philosopher Arthur Holmes assumed leadership of the faith and learning seminars, producing a "Holmes Project" that drew inspiration from Henry. He viewed integration as imperative for a college that aspired to be distinctly Christian; thus he challenged new faculty to relate Scripture and theology to their disciplines. As he expressed it, "integration is ultimately concerned to see things whole from a Christian perspective, to penetrate thought with that perspective, to think Christianly."[39] His approach to integration gained many supporters in the Consortium and the Coalition; in fact, he continues even now to assist the CCCU with workshops for new faculty.

Finally, the Dutch Reformed model of integration that has characterized Calvin College represents a sometimes unacknowledged stream of influence. Like Henry and Holmes, scholars at Calvin have stressed the importance of worldview and genuinely Christian thinking. Philosopher Nicholas Wolterstorff, who taught at Calvin for several years before heading to Yale, spoke at Richard Chase's inauguration as president of Wheaton in 1982 in language that echoes Holmes: "The calling of the Christian scholar is to practice scholarship in Christian perspective and to penetrate to the roots of that scholarship with which she finds herself in disagreement—along the way appropriating whatever she finds of use."[40] At the same time, Dutch Reformed thought about faith and learning was thoroughly Kuyperian. Abraham Kuyper, who founded the Free University of Amsterdam in 1880 and served as prime minister of the Netherlands in the early twentieth century, affirmed the Lordship of Christ over all creation, the cultural mandate, the pervasiveness of sin in all human endeavor, and the substantial gap between the fundamental assumptions of Christian and non-Christian scholarship. Apart from Wolterstorff's involvement in the faith and learning institutes, it is difficult to find abundant evidence of Kuyperian perspectives in the early Consortium. They began to surface when Gordon Werkema, who attended Calvin College for three years, accepted the leadership of the Consortium in 1974; ultimately their influence peaked in the Coalition during the 1980s.[41]

In the analysis of James Hendrix, Werkema accented "the distinctive philosophic mission of evangelical colleges."[42] Therefore, it is not surprising to learn that efforts by the Consortium to encourage the integration of faith and learning intensified during his tenure at the helm. Werkema also figured prominently in the creation of a new association, which is the subject of the next chapter. The Christian College Coalition eventually would inherit some of the integration legacy that had been nurtured so well by its parent organization.

THREE

The Birth of the American Studies Program and the Christian College Coalition

~~~~~

Gordon Werkema

On the basis of the recommendation from a search committee chaired by David McKenna, the Christian College Consortium appointed Gordon Werkema as its new executive director, effective June 1, 1974. In accepting this post, Werkema became the Consortium's first full-time professional employee. Prior to this, he served as the assistant executive director of the Council for the Advancement of Small Colleges (CASC) in Washington, D.C., so the Consortium decided to relocate its national office to that city. At Werkema's request, the nomenclature of his title was changed to "president" in early 1975.[1]

After attending Calvin College for three years, Werkema had earned his bachelor's, master's, and doctoral degrees at the University of Denver. A product of the Christian school movement, he had developed an interest in legal issues pertaining to private schools, including parental rights. This may explain why he also took some classes at the University of Wyoming School of Law. Before working with CASC, he was president of Trinity Christian College, an institution with Christian Reformed ties near Chicago.[2]

A relatively young man of thirty-seven at the time of his Consortium appointment, Werkema brought a good deal of energy to the position. He has been variously described as "an educational entrepreneur," "a visionary," and "an idea man."[3] In his three years as president, Werkema conceived and instituted several Consortium projects, including a marketing action program, a legal advisory network, faculty exchanges between member institutions, the Christian College News Service, and the Christian University Press; the latter was a cooperative venture between the Consortium and William B. Eerdmans Publishing Company to encourage excellence in Christian scholarship.[4] In retrospect, however, Werkema's greatest contributions involved his leadership in two virtually simultaneous initiatives, the American Studies Program and the Christian College Coalition.

The American Studies Program

In early 1975 Gordon Werkema reported to the Consortium that a proposal for the establishment of an American Studies Center in Washington was "in the final stages of development."[5] The Consortium president envisioned an innovative one-semester program for political science, American history, and other majors from member schools. Students would reside on Capitol Hill, participate in a modular American studies course, engage in independent study, and complete internships.[6] Werkema labored diligently with the Consortium Deans' Council, which was established in 1972, to gain approval for this experimental venture. The Deans' Council saw great potential in the program and initially agreed to a January 1976 start date, which was later changed to September 1976.[7]

To direct the American Studies Program (ASP), the Consortium tapped John Bernbaum, whom Werkema had once interviewed for a teaching position at Trinity Christian College. Bernbaum had studied as an undergraduate at Trinity Christian and Calvin, had completed a Ph.D. in European and Russian history at the University of Maryland, and had spent four years in the United States Foreign Service. When he renewed acquaintances with Werkema at Fourth Presbyterian Church in the Washington area, Bernbaum was employed as a historian and contributing editor for the Foreign Relations of the United

States series at the State Department. Bernbaum really desired to teach, so Werkema talked with him about the ASP possibility. After an interview with the Deans' Council, Bernbaum was hired to run the new program. Since the Council had authorized the ASP on a one-year trial basis, Bernbaum took a temporary leave from his government position, although he realized within three months in his new position that he would not be returning to "Foggy Bottom."[8]

As the Jimmy Carter–Gerald Ford presidential race heated up in the fall of 1976, the ASP opened its doors to nineteen students, somewhat lower than the original goal of twenty-five. The program was originally housed at Thompson-Markward Hall, a residence for Christian women at 235 Second Street NE, in Washington. This facility provided a floor to house male students, a wing for female students, and office and classroom space in the basement. Although Thompson-Markward Hall had limited space for expansion of the ASP, it nevertheless allowed for "a sense of Christian community."[9]

Werkema and Bernbaum both emphasized that the learning experiences in the ASP held great potential for cultural engagement and the integration of faith and learning. In perhaps the best illustration of how a Kuyperian model influenced the Consortium, these two men vigorously defended the legitimacy of Christian participation in government and politics. Bernbaum approached his mission in the ASP with the hope of encouraging "the best and the brightest" Christian young people to pursue careers in public service.[10] In planning for the ASP, Werkema argued that one of its most attractive aspects would be a greater awareness by faculty and students of "the opportunities Christians have for ministry and service in the government, national life, and public policy development."[11] As students examined topics such as Congress, the National Security Council, evangelical political activism, and the arts in American culture, Bernbaum passionately challenged them "to integrate Christianity with all areas of life instead of compartmentalizing it off in a corner."[12]

After one year, close to fifty students from fifteen colleges had participated in the ASP, and the Deans' Council voted to remove its "temporary" status. Werkema pronounced the endeavor a practical and philosophical success:

> The American Studies Program . . . is one of, if not the most, significant programs we have begun in my opinion. Interviews with students have consistently emphasized the fact that their Christian faith has been

strengthened, their understanding of national life deepened, and the possibility of integration of faith, learning, and living a contemporary Christian life made real. Interviews with intern supervisors have emphasized the fact that there are many in the bureaucracies, etc., who are being exposed to the products of Christian liberal arts colleges with renewed appreciation for the quality of students we have within our colleges. When the program was being planned I do not believe that we recognized that this program would meet so many of the Consortium's original objectives.[13]

Werkema's enthusiastic vision and Bernbaum's creative leadership certainly proved to be an effective combination in getting the ASP off to a running start.

As Marge Bernbaum, who assisted her husband on a part-time basis, expressed it, the ASP quickly became a "flagship" for what the Consortium was trying to accomplish on behalf of Christian higher education.[14] In fact, the ASP plan guided Werkema as he developed additional proposals for student programs in Latin America and the Far East. Even though he announced his resignation in July of 1977, Werkema continued to frame the Latin American project, hoping that it could be launched in the fall of 1978. He and Carl Lundquist, president of Bethel College in Minnesota, arranged a working relationship with Universidad Mariano Galvez de Guatemala that would allow students from Consortium colleges to live and study in Central America. Despite the promise of this intercultural program, the Deans' Council recommended in June of 1978 that it be cancelled "due to little interest."[15] The Far East initiative, which was in an even more preliminary stage, also was aborted after Werkema's departure from the Consortium.[16] As will be seen in succeeding chapters, both of these programming ideas resurfaced later in the Christian College Coalition.

A New Organization: The Christian College Coalition

Since control of the American Studies Program ultimately shifted from the Consortium to the Christian College Coalition, the birth of the subsidiary association points to another important dimension of Gordon Werkema's Consortium leadership. As he drew up plans for the ASP, Werkema was well aware of membership issues facing the Consortium; Richard Stephens, former president of Greenville College, has called this the "subterranean problem."[17] Other evangelical colleges desired to join the Consortium, but the presidents of Consortium schools showed a marked reluctance to let the organization expand. Leaders at aspiring but jilted institutions thus perceived the Consortium colleges as elitist, even suggesting that the Consortium was little more than a "presidents' club." Houghton College president Daniel Chamberlain, who was academic dean at Messiah until 1976, gingerly summarized the problem of external pressure for membership growth:

> The Consortium resisted that pressure because we believed we could accomplish some things as a small group which we could not do if we were much larger. We also faced the pragmatic issue of establishing appropriate criteria for new members. The Consortium would have been happy to add some colleges but reluctant to add many others. The group was frequently attacked as elitist and we believed that highly selective additions would add to the frequency, and perhaps even the legitimacy, of such attacks.[18]

Chamberlain's comments only hinted at the question of doctrinal and behavioral membership standards, which concerned Hudson Armerding of Wheaton. In particular, Armerding opposed allowing colleges into the Consortium that admitted non-Christian students as an evangelistic strategy. The Wheaton president, like several of his colleagues, had also come to appreciate the fellowship and camaraderie that were vital parts of their Consortium meetings.[19] Hence, the creation of a new agency might remove the pressure for the Consortium to expand while preserving its original character and ethos.

Another key motivation for organizing the Coalition was what David McKenna terms the "threat factor."[20] In the 1970s Christian colleges confronted a cluster of sensitive church/state issues relating to both federal aid and regulation. For example, the Supreme Court case *Tilton v. Richardson* (1971) established the principle, which was later invoked in similar cases, that federal assistance could be granted to church-related institutions that were not "pervasively religious."[21] In the area of legislation, Title IX of the Education Amendments of 1972 prohibited discrimination against women and required written certification of compliance, even from schools where the only federal aid that was accepted went directly to students. This caused problems for Grove City College, a Christian institution that philosophically refused to verify adherence to Title IX because it did not receive direct federal assistance.[22] Finally, a Cabinet-level Department of Education loomed on the horizon, suggesting the possibility of even more intrusive federal regulation.[23]

To respond effectively to these challenges and to defend their interests in Washington, the Christian college movement required more clout than could be generated by the fourteen members of the Consortium. Further, as Bethel (Minnesota) president George Brushaber observed, the Consortium had not initially spelled out its objectives with a public policy role in mind.[24] Thus, in terms of both size and mission, the Consortium was not disposed to assume significant lobbying activities in the nation's capital.

At a Consortium executive committee meeting in January 1975, David McKenna raised the threat issue, urging the Consortium to develop a policy regarding the religious freedom and "purpose base" of member institutions. The committee then approved McKenna's motion that Gordon Werkema study the matter and present a proposal at a February planning retreat.[25] Among his five-year projections, Werkema recommended that the Consortium form a "Council of or for Christian Colleges" as an association that would be owned and operated by the Consortium's board of directors. The Consortium president outlined the proposed council's objectives as: (1) "the provision of specified services"; (2) "the enhancement of promotion and leadership activities for Christian higher education by providing larger resources and representational bases"; (3) "the development of a unified voice for evangelical Christian higher education"; and (4) "the stimulation of greater attention to basic issues in Christian higher education."[26] Perhaps because Werkema stated the goals in rather general terms, Consortium leaders did not act immediately on his proposal. Instead, the board of directors requested in March 1975 that Werkema prepare a more detailed prospectus to be considered at an October meeting.[27]

Between March and October, Werkema refined both the rationale for and aims of a new council. His report to the Consortium board stressed the urgency of a cooperative effort by "those interested in religiously integrated values in higher education" because "no one in the nation now focuses their attention on that group, certainly not from an evangelical Christian perspective." He then suggested that the subsidiary organization be called either "the Council of Christian Colleges" or "the Christian College Coalition," and that its agenda include the

ickly pointed out that the NAICU "will not represent us adequately
those critical areas that make us a special interest group."[33] One of
ose critical areas that required a unified voice was the integration of
th and learning: "It is apparent to sensitive observers that the per-
ation of one's educational philosophy with religious belief will be
estioned as to its legitimacy more and more in an increasingly sec-
ar society."[34] On that account, the Consortium desired to protect a
y distinctive of its own by weaving it into the public advocacy agenda
the Coalition.

On September 21 and 22, 1976, the Christian College Coalition
ld its organizational meeting on Capitol Hill in Washington. Not far
ay on Second Street, the Consortium's American Studies Program
s in its first semester of operation. The broader evangelical move-
nt, with which the Consortium and Coalition identified, basked in
light of unusual media attention, caused in part by the openly born-
in profession of the Democratic presidential candidate, Jimmy
ter. Indeed, the Coalition's founding occurred in what *Newsweek*
gazine declared to be "the Year of the Evangelicals."[35] Given the
itically-charged context of an election year, it is interesting that
rkema invited Chuck Colson, who was converted to Christ while
ving prison time in the aftermath of the Watergate scandal, to speak
he meeting. Werkema believes that this may have been Colson's
: public address after his release from prison.[36]

residents from twenty-six Christian colleges attended the Coali-
's initial gathering; this number included the fourteen Consortium
itutions, all of whom pledged to join the Coalition. Twelve addi-
al schools, which were unable to participate in the September meet-
also committed to the Coalition shortly thereafter. Thus, the Coali-
essentially started with thirty-eight members.[37] Coalition
nbership mirrored the denominational pluralism of both evangel-
sm and the Consortium. Among those early joiners that were not
e Consortium and have maintained continuous Coalition/CCCU
nbership since 1976, the following denominations were repre-
ed: American Baptist (Eastern, Judson); Southern Baptist (Camp-
ville); Presbyterian Church in America (Covenant); Reformed Pres-
rian (Geneva); Grace Brethren (Grace); Wesleyan (Marion);
mblies of God (Evangel); and Christian and Missionary Alliance
ck, Simpson). Further, the Coalition included several independ-
olleges (Azusa Pacific, Biola, Bryan, and John Brown).

following: (1) "the monitoring of legislation, judicial ac
lic opinion on matters which could affect the freedom o
leges to function educationally and religiously;" (2) "th
of unified positions on critical issues for presentation
izations, governmental bodies, and public policy forme
development of an offensive position on potential erosi
and educational freedom in the Christian college move
Werkema envisioned a much larger advocacy role for
ation than was the case with the Consortium up to th

Werkema believed that a council or coalition cou
125 members "if orthodox, Protestant, and conservativ
applied." He also advised an annual membership fee
would provide legal counsel, workshops, and consu
gious liberty issues, as well as reduced rates
Faith/Learning/Living Institutes. Finally, Werkema p
president of the Consortium serve concurrently as the
subsidiary, with the proviso that an executive associa
the new group reached a membership of seventy-five.
utive was to lead both organizations, the Coalition,
Consortium's staff and office facilities, at that time
Massachusetts Avenue NE, in Washington.[30]

For almost a year, the Consortium worked to bui
new venture, even as it was likewise promoting the
January 1976, the name Christian College Coalition
and a description sheet based on Werkema's prospe
ous October had been prepared for distribution to
colleges.[31] Werkema's report in March to the Consor
ing indicated that response to the mailing was "mi
he still hoped to launch the Coalition in the spring.[32]
to be overly optimistic; apparently several Christian
more coaxing to participate in the Coalition.

In July 1976 the Consortium released an inforn
Coalition that was obviously designed to answer
about membership. This four-page document anr
ber organizational meeting, listed colleges that had
and provided additional information on fees, bu
programs. The Consortium also encouraged Chris
ticipate in another new higher educational ende
Association of Independent Colleges and Universi

The diverse group that convened in Washington learned about the Coalition's purposes, functions, organization, and relationships. The conference also offered several sessions on public policy matters: "Introduction to the Legal System as It Relates to Colleges," led by Werkema; "How to Build a Relationship with Your Congressman and Senator and His Office," conducted by Burnett Thompson, a government relations consultant for the Consortium; and "Current Legal Issues Confronting Christian Higher Education," directed by John Myers and Bruce Hopkins from the law firm that the Consortium was using for legal counsel.[38] Finally, organizational items occupied part of the schedule, including the approval of the previously expressed Coalition objectives and the election of the first board. The board consisted of the following institutional presidents: Robert Baptista (Taylor), Richard Chase (Biola), David LeShana (George Fox), Robert Luckey (Marion, later renamed Indiana Wesleyan), Carl Lundquist (Bethel), and Daniel Weiss (Eastern).[39] The organizing board therefore drew equally from Consortium and new Coalition schools, perhaps in reaction to what Werkema described as "a great deal of unhappiness about limited membership" in the Consortium and "some expressed concerns about the desire of the Consortium to control the Coalition."[40] Little did the early Coalition members know in 1976 that the relationship between the two organizations would change dramatically within a five-year period.

On November 23, 1976, the Coalition board met in Indianapolis to conduct necessary business and chart the new association's first year. In a flurry of activity, the board (1) elected Richard Chase of Biola as its chair; (2) appropriated a 1976–77 budget for Coalition activities of $26,600, which was part of the overall Consortium budget; (3) decided to establish an annual workshop to be held in Washington in late January; (4) reached consensus on the Coalition's purposes, procedures, and objectives that generally fell in line with earlier proposals and discussions; (5) agreed to develop a statement on governmental regulation; (6) asked Werkema to prepare a handbook to assist colleges in dealing with threats to religious liberty; and (7) set up procedures for providing legal counsel to member colleges.[41]

A follow-up meeting in New Orleans on February 11, 1977, was held in conjunction with an NAICU gathering. Here the board approved bylaws that Werkema and Chase had prepared, decided on the title "Legal and Governmental Issues for Christian Colleges" for the proposed handbook, and revised a statement on "Government Relations, Financial Support, and Regulation of Christian Colleges." This position paper encompassed many of the Coalition's vital concerns, including the legitimacy of independent colleges, the need for freedom of choice in educational matters, and the desirability of responsible governmental deregulation of higher education.[42]

Legal and governmental issues obviously dominated the documents and meetings of the Coalition during its organizing phase. By March 1977, Werkema reported that the primary motive for institutions joining the Coalition was "to participate in a group which will help preserve their educational distinctives and protect the right of the college to develop, administer, and implement its own Christian philosophy."[43] While this early agenda definitely reflected a principal aim of the Consortium in creating a subsidiary group, it is not entirely clear that Werkema relished the more overtly political role that would be necessary to solidify the Coalition's presence in Washington.[44] He functioned best as an idea man, educator, and organizer. After supervising the successful inauguration of the ASP and the Coalition, he evidently felt that it was time for a change. Werkema resigned his position effective October 31, 1977, and became executive vice president at Seattle Pacific University, where David McKenna was still president.[45] New leadership would soon be in place as the Consortium/Coalition entered a new era of its history.

FOUR

Advancing the Cause in and beyond the Nation's Capital

———

John Dellenback

Following Gordon Werkema's resignation as Consortium/Coalition president, a search committee headed by Ray Hostetter, president of Messiah College, began the process of finding a replacement. Mark Hatfield, the Republican senator from Oregon, recommended that the committee consider John Dellenback, a former congressman from the same state. The committee interviewed Dellenback, and was favorably impressed with his background and Christian commitment. David Winter, president of Westmont College and a member of the search committee, recently recalled that as the committee neared the end of their interview with Dellenback, the only remaining question concerned lifestyle issues (e.g., dancing and drinking). The candidate quipped that he was a poor dancer, but that he sometimes drank wine with meals. Moreover, it was reported that when Dellenback first met with a group of presidents from member institutions, he jokingly apologized that his wife Mary Jane could not be present due to a tap dancing lesson. The committee members unanimously endorsed him and the Consortium's board of directors ratified their choice. On November 1, 1977, Dellenback assumed his presidential duties at the Consortium/Coalition office, then located at 11 Dupont Circle NE, in Washington.[1]

Dellenback brought impressive credentials to his new position. A Phi Beta Kappa graduate of Yale, he later received his law degree from the University of Michigan. He attained the rank of lieutenant commander in the U.S. Navy, practiced as an attorney, pursued business interests, and taught business law at Oregon State University. In 1961 Dellenback stepped into state politics as a Republican delegate to the Oregon legislature. He then served Oregon's fourth congressional district for four terms (1967–75) in the U.S. House of Representatives, where he was a member of the Education and Labor Committee. After losing a reelection bid in 1974, when Richard Nixon's Watergate problems hurt many GOP candidates, Dellenback accepted an appointment from President Gerald Ford in 1975 to direct the Peace Corps. His tenure at the Peace Corps ended early in 1977 with the accession of Democrat Jimmy Carter to the White House.[2] Several months later, Dellenback emerged as the leading prospect for the Consortium/Coalition presidency.

The Consortium and Coalition shared Dellenback's leadership for about four years. Even after that, his part-time salary masked the fact that he was employed full time with the Coalition. Nonetheless, his managerial style emphasized teamwork, delegation of significant autonomy to staff, and a strong relational approach.[3] Many of Dellenback's staffers admired his enthusiastic yet gentle leadership and came to regard him as a valued mentor.[4] He handled financial matters with some degree of informality; an unselfish person, he on occasion balanced the Coalition budget by writing a personal check.[5]

Since the Coalition's initial objectives focused especially on the protection of the religious and educational freedom of faith-affirming colleges, it was expected that Dellenback would devote considerable energy to such issues. Although staff had to bring him up to speed on the world of Christian higher education,[6] Dellenback moved with ease through the corridors of power in Washington, a fact that certainly influenced the decision to hire him in the first place. He stayed busy with legal and governmental concerns, if only because some problems that set off alarms in the 1970s remained unresolved well into the 1980s. Moreover, all colleges and universities had to confront the reality of reductions in federal aid to students during the Reagan years.[7]

As a statesman with significant stature in Washington, Dellenback took advantage of his contacts in Congress and the federal bureaucracies. He also looked for opportunities to promote Christian higher education in the capital. He developed a Coalition relationship with the Center for Constitutional Studies, which allowed colleges to channel legal questions to the Center through Dellenback.[8] In addition, he understood the value of working with other higher educational agencies in Washington. By 1980 he sat on the National Association of Independent Colleges and Universities Secretariat, the NAICU Government Relations Advisory Council, the Church Denominational Educational Executives Council, and the steering committee for the church-related colleges of the American Association of Presidents of Independent Colleges and Universities.[9] Both the Consortium and the Coalition clearly benefited from a widening circle of influence that Dellenback was cultivating.

On the legal front, the Coalition relied on Dellenback's expertise to help defend Christian colleges against unwarranted governmental encroachment. In 1979 Dellenback and Bruce Hopkins, the Coalition's legal counsel, prepared and filed an *amicus curiae* brief in a Circuit Court of Appeals on behalf of Mississippi College, a Coalition member. A former part-time faculty member sued the Southern Baptist institution, charging that she was refused a full-time position on the basis of gender. The college, contra the Equal Employment Opportunity Commission, saw this as a religious liberty issue and successfully insisted on the right to require a meaningful Christian commitment from all full-time professors. In the brief, Dellenback and Hopkins cited the First Amendment and Title VII of the Civil Rights Act of 1964, concluding that "anything which threatens the freedom of committed Christian colleges to select their faculties on the basis of the presence of these (moral and religious convictions) in a fundamental and inevitable way threatens the basic purposes and mission of these institutions."[10]

The Coalition also supported Grove City College, which was then a member, in its battle with the federal government over Title IX. In particular, Dellenback strongly affirmed the school's position that "federal assistance given to a student is not to be considered as federal aid to the institution that student attends."[11] Dellenback and Senator Mark Hatfield sought a legislative remedy for Grove City in 1980, hoping to amend the Higher Education Act reauthorization so that it would distinguish between aid to a student and aid to an institution. The Hatfield Amendment failed, and the Supreme Court eventually decided the Grove City case in 1984. The Court ruled that aid to a student constituted assistance to an institution, but also declared that Title IX only applied to the specific programs or activities where aid was received.[12]

While the Grove City case was making its way to the Supreme Court, the Coalition established a committee on government relations and legal issues. Key members included: Eugene Habecker, president of Huntington College, who served as the first chairman; Richard Stephens, president of Greenville College, who had experience testifying before congressional committees on educational issues; and John Brown III, president of John Brown University, who was also an attorney. This committee entered into working relationships with the Christian Legal Society and NAICU, kept the Coalition informed about pending litigation, and offered Dellenback additional resources for dealing with political and legal matters.[13]

While threat issues figured so prominently in the Coalition's founding and early history, Dellenback undoubtedly entertained a broader vision for what the association could be doing. Under his direction, the Coalition became much different in mission and scope than was even hinted at in the original objectives. The magnitude of this shift did not become clear until Dellenback initiated steps to change the basic relationship between the Coalition and its parent organization, the Consortium.

The Coalition and the Consortium Separate

Almost from the beginning, the Consortium/Coalition distinction and its accompanying division of responsibilities posed problems in the areas of morale, logistics, and public perception. For his part, Dellenback preferred the Coalition part of his job description and saw the real future of the Christian college movement there.[14] At Dellenback's behest, the Coalition's board of directors and the Consortium's executive board discussed the relationship between the two organizations at meetings in Chicago in October 1980. The Coalition board commissioned its chairman, Daniel Weiss of Eastern College, to form a task force that would examine the Coalition's future from a number of perspectives. The very next day, the Consortium's executive committee was told that the Coalition was exploring the possibility of separating from the parent group.[15]

In March 1981, presidents of the Consortium member schools met in Bermuda for a retreat. Lon Randall, president of Malone College, presented a report on Coalition planning, noting that its task force was investigating name, purpose, budget, office staff relationships, potential separation from the Consortium, and other matters. Following a lengthy discussion, the Consortium leaders approved a motion "to encourage the Executive Committee of the Coalition and its membership to establish a separate entity." The motion included a pledge of "our support and desire to cooperate on matters of finance, executive leadership, and program coordination."[16] While many details still needed attention, the Consortium seemed genuinely supportive of the Coalition's move toward legal independence.

Later that same month the separation issue dominated the Consortium executive committee meeting in Washington. Dellenback made it clear that he wanted to serve the Coalition, drop his Consortium duties, and consider other possible options for professional growth and service to fill the time that he was currently devoting to the Consortium. Then he reported that the Coalition eagerly desired to broaden its purposes to include program development, "without diluting its goal of monitoring and influencing legislation, regulations and litigations."[17] It is not evident from the minutes whether Dellenback at this point sought to bring the American Studies Program into the Coalition, even though his statement of purpose at least hinted at such a move. The executive committee discussion, however, focused primarily on questions about Consortium leadership and location of headquarters after separation. Committee members expressed a consensus that the Coalition remain in the Washington office, located at 1776 Massachusetts Avenue NE, while "the Consortium headquarters should be where the leadership is presently working; probably on a college campus where a president or former president resides." Consequently, the committee asked Daniel Chamberlain of Houghton College to poll Consortium presidents about naming Carl Lundquist, who was nearing retirement from Bethel College and Seminary, as the new Consortium executive.[18]

By the time of the Coalition board meeting in May 1981, the process of legal separation from the Consortium was well underway. In addition, the issue of the American Studies Program surfaced when Dellenback reported that an Oregon donor was considering a $500,000 gift to the Coalition for the purchase of an available building on Fourth

Street NE, that was needed for ASP offices and student housing. Technically, of course, the ASP still belonged to the Consortium; hence, Dan Chamberlain moved that the Coalition assume control of the ASP, a motion that passed unanimously. There were several other motions regarding the receipt of the gift and the necessary steps to establish the Coalition as an IRS tax-exempt corporation.[19]

All that remained was for the Consortium to grant its blessing to the actions taken by the Coalition board. The Consortium directors met in Chicago on June 3, 1981. Chairman Chamberlain, who was also on the Coalition board, asked Dellenback to present a report on a gift of fifteen shares of common capital stock in Sierra Cascade Communications from Mr. and Mrs. J. L. DeArmond, Dellenback's friends from Oregon. Dellenback then outlined the distribution of the gift, which was summarized in the minutes as follows:

> Ten percent for the Christian College Consortium for such use as its Board of Directors shall determine, the remaining 90 percent to be used for the support of the American Studies Program in whatever fashion as shall be decided upon by the Board of Directors of the Christian College Coalition. It is hoped that the Coalition would utilize the funds to acquire and maintain a building for student housing.[20]

Since the DeArmond gift held major implications for the future of the Consortium, it is not surprising that the directors discussed at some length. Finally, the board voted to approve the Coalition request to take over the ASP and to authorize Dellenback to take the necessary legal actions to accept the gift and secure the new property, which became known as the DeArmond House.[21]

The DeArmond gift represented a stunning coup for Dellenback and the Coalition, albeit one that engendered some sharp criticism. Chamberlain, who helped to smooth the way for the momentous changes with both the Consortium and Coalition boards, recently recollected that Dellenback solicited the bequest without the awareness or explicit approval of his boards.[22] Nonetheless, Consortium presidents generally supported the conditions attached to the gift, probably recognizing that the Coalition offered a larger network of support and that the Consortium would face a difficult time operating the ASP with its headquarters removed from Washington. Some Consortium deans, who had nurtured and supervised the ASP, responded to Dellenback's moves with an undisguised resentment; indeed, they perceived that the ASP had been "stolen" from them.[23] Part of the problem with the deans no doubt stemmed from their perception that Dellenback's modus operandi in this matter reflected his lack of experience in academic decision making.[24] Furthermore, when the deans realized that their impending loss of the ASP was irreversible, their frustration only intensified.

The events of 1981 significantly altered both organizations. In October 1981, the Consortium board duly elected Carl Lundquist as its president, with the understanding that he would serve one-quarter time his first year and one-half time after that.[25] He subsequently moved the national office to St. Paul, Minnesota, where he continued to lead the Consortium until ill health forced his resignation in 1990. Although the Consortium scaled back its programs, Pew Charitable Trust grants in the middle and late 1980s allowed for new interdisciplinary initiatives in the humanities and faculty development. Since 1991 Thomas Englund has headed the Consortium on a part-time basis from his home in Dunbarton, New Hampshire.[26]

By the time that John Dellenback filed incorporation papers in the District of Columbia on January 28, 1982, the Coalition was already positioned to occupy a strategic place in the world of Christian higher education.[27] All the Consortium colleges retained their memberships in the Coalition, but the younger organization no longer functioned in the shadow of its parent. In fact, the size, scope, and resources of the Coalition had grown substantially in just over five years to the extent that it now dwarfed the Consortium. The upward growth pattern turned out to be another key component of Dellenback's vision.

The Critical Mass

Dellenback probably would have confronted major hurdles in moving the Coalition toward independence and control of the American Studies Program if he had not already been working to expand the association's base. He firmly believed that the Coalition needed to build a "critical mass" of Christian colleges before it could be effective in Washington. The seriousness with which he pursued this task is evident in the extensive typewritten lists of prospective members that he maintained in a file. One list was even color-coded with markers to help distinguish potential member schools from others that were unlikely to join.[28] Dellenback also traveled to the campuses of at least a dozen institutions that he hoped might join the Coalition.[29]

In response to Dellenback's concern that some Christian colleges might not be a good fit, the Coalition developed membership criteria to ensure that only "Christ-centered" schools would be eligible. The organization looked for the following before granting admission: (1) accreditation as a four-year liberal arts college; (2) institutional commitment to Christ; (3) a policy of hiring well-qualified faculty and administrators who were committed Christians; (4) commitment to the integration of faith, learning, and living; and (5) commitment to excellence.[30] Thus, the desire to enlarge the Coalition did not override the importance of maintaining genuinely Christian distinctives.

During Dellenback's presidency, the Coalition more than doubled its membership. When he assumed leadership in 1977, membership had dipped to thirty-one; when he retired in 1988, there were seventy-seven institutions in the Coalition. To encourage his staff members, Dellenback and his wife took them out for dinner when membership hit the round numbers of forty, fifty, sixty, and seventy.[31]

As the organization expanded, it continued to be marked by denominational pluralism. Members that joined for the first time during the Dellenback years represented several Protestant traditions: Bartlesville Wesleyan and Southern Wesleyan (Wesleyan); Roberts Wesleyan and Spring Arbor (Free Methodist); Eastern Nazarene, Mt. Vernon Nazarene, Northwest Nazarene, Olivet Nazarene, Point Loma Nazarene, Southern Nazarene, and Trevecca Nazarene (Church of the Nazarene); Sioux Falls (American Baptist); Dallas Baptist, Campbell, and Palm Beach Atlantic (Southern Baptist); Belhaven, Sterling, and Whitworth (Presbyterian); Calvin and Dordt (Christian Reformed); Northwestern of Iowa (Reformed Church in America); Goshen (Mennonite); Fresno Pacific and Tabor (Mennonite Brethren); Bethel of Kansas (General Conference Mennonite); Warner Pacific and Warner Southern (Church of God, Anderson, Indiana); Milligan (Christian Church/Churches of Christ); Northwest Christian (Disciples of Christ); Vanguard, then Southern California College (Assemblies of God); Lee (Church of God, Cleveland Tennessee); Huntington (United Brethren in Christ); and Bethel of Indiana (Missionary Church). The Coalition also embraced additional independent schools like Colorado Christian, LeTourneau, the Master's College (then Los Angeles Baptist College), Northwestern of Minnesota, Oral Roberts, and Trinity Christian, some of which had informal denominational ties. Finally, the first Canadian institutions were accepted in the mid-1980s: Redeemer of Ontario (independent), which became the seventy-fifth member in 1986; Trinity Western of British Columbia (Evangelical Free); and the King's University College of Alberta (also independent).[32]

The process of developing the critical mass ran into some snags. Applications from Liberty University and Oral Roberts generated extensive debate in Coalition board meetings, primarily because of their founders' notoriety and fundraising techniques.[33] While Liberty was never admitted, Oral Roberts came in for a period, was asked to withdraw, and later rejoined. Dellenback, whose non-sectarian and ecumenical spirit certainly helped to boost membership, also attempted unsuccessfully to recruit Missouri Synod and Churches of Christ (non-instrumental) institutions.[34] By almost every measure, however, he left office in 1988 with the satisfaction that the critical mass had been achieved.

Student Programs and Staff

John Bernbaum continued to direct the American Studies Program; he was in agreement with the change of sponsorship in 1981–82 and made a smooth transition from the Consortium to the Coalition.[35] While the basic structure and philosophy of the ASP remained the same, some fine-tuning strengthened it. Innovations during the Dellenback years included a special January interterm, Washington seminars for faculty of member institutions, and a summer internship program.[36]

Bernbaum also benefited from some new staff. Rich Gathro, a product of Trinity College (now Trinity International University) in Illinois, started working part time for the ASP in 1978, while still maintaining a position with National Student Leadership. At first, his main responsibility was to find internships for the students. In 1980, however, he accepted a full-time post with the ASP as associate director, combining both teaching and administration. He later enhanced his academic credentials by completing a master's in theological studies in 1981 at Wesley Theological Seminary, where he wrote a thesis on the British evangelical politician William Wilberforce. Over the years, Gathro has contributed significantly to the Coalition/CCCU, and currently serves as senior vice president.[37]

Bernbaum gained another ASP faculty member and associate director in 1981 when Jerry Herbert, former director of the Carolina Study

Center, moved with his family to Washington. Herbert, who earned a Ph.D. in political science at Duke University, previously had met Bernbaum at a conference on the campus of Dordt College. That contact led to an invitation to teach in two different January interterms for the ASP before he came on full time. Through the Dellenback years, he and his family lived with ASP students in a rented building on Capitol Hill. In addition to teaching, Herbert also performed administrative functions and, in 1992, became director of the ASP.[38]

The ASP proudly celebrated its tenth anniversary with a three-day reunion in May of 1986. By this time over nine hundred students had been through the program, and many returned for the occasion. Bernbaum remarked that alumni testimonies represented "a reaffirmation of what we're doing here."[39] A different type of recognition came the following year, when an *Eternity* magazine interview featured the work of Gathro and Herbert at the ASP.[40]

The ASP also served as a model for the long-awaited Latin American Studies Program (LASP). Originally conceived as a Consortium project toward the end of the Werkema era, the LASP received fresh life when the Coalition board authorized an ASP proposal for a feasibility study early in 1985.[41] During the next several months, Bernbaum solicited input from professors at Coalition colleges, as well as from Latin American experts in Christian organizations and the U.S. government. The ASP director also journeyed to Latin America, where he consulted with educators and representatives of Christian groups. In the fall of 1985, Bernbaum presented a proposal to the Coalition board for a program to be based in San Jose, Costa Rica. Bernbaum anticipated that LASP students would live with Costa Rican families, gain practical experience in internships, attend seminars and language class, and travel to other Latin American countries. The board enthusiastically approved this program to start within a year.[42]

Roland Hoksbergen, an economics professor at Calvin College, accepted the Coalition call to direct the LASP. Earlier he had ministered in Central America with the Christian Reformed World Relief Committee; moreover, his wife Lisseth was Guatemalan.[43] He inaugurated the Coalition's first international program with ten students in the fall of 1986, ten years after the ASP was launched. For the new director, the LASP offered "a special opportunity for students to understand the Kingdom of God from the perspective of the developing world while also increasing their understanding of another culture."[44] The subsequent success of the LASP in turn sparked other Coalition/CCCU intercultural ventures under later presidents.

Faculty Development

After separation from the Consortium, faculty development emerged as a new Coalition priority, one that had initially been carried on a limited basis by the parent organization. Karen Longman, who began employment with the Consortium/Coalition as Dellenback's program assistant in 1980, ultimately became the key facilitator in this area. She had developed an interest in faculty development as a Ph.D. student in higher education at the University of Michigan. Her dissertation research on faculty growth contracts took her to eight institutions, some of which were Christian. Rich Gathro set up an appointment for her to talk with John Dellenback, and the Consortium/Coalition president hired her at first to do general research, assist in fundraising, keep alert to relevant federal policy issues, and supervise the operation of the Christian University Press. In a position whose responsibilities evolved over time, Longman began to devote increasing attention to faculty development issues.[45]

Before the Coalition put its own faculty programs in place, it endorsed Trinity College's Faith/Learning/Living Institute, held for three successive summers (1979–81) at the school's campus in Deerfield, Illinois. Kenneth Shipps, a professor of history at Trinity, directed what Longman described as "the only long-term national conference for faculty members involving both disciplinary study and interdisciplinary sessions."[46] The 1981 Trinity institute impressed Longman enough that she began to work with Shipps on a grant proposal to the National Endowment for the Humanities (NEH). They hoped to gain funding for a series of Coalition workshops on the relationship of the humanities to the Christian faith.[47]

In July of 1982 the NEH announced a two-year, $135,000 grant to the Coalition for ten week-long regional workshops and a four-week interdisciplinary national institute. The NEH program officer, who was a Roman Catholic, engaged in some light-hearted humor when she remarked, "It's good to know that God hears the prayers of the Protestants!"[48] The workshops were specifically designed to promote the integration of faith and learning, the development of curricular materials in particular disciplines, and the overall improvement of the teaching of the humanities at Coalition colleges. The grant allowed 150 faculty from Coalition schools to participate in the workshops and institutes.[49]

The NEH funding seemed to open the door for additional faculty development grants. Early in 1984 the M. J. Murdock Charitable Trust of Vancouver, Washington, awarded the Coalition a $60,000 grant to fund a summer conference for business and economics professors.[50] Then, after the NEH declined to fund a second series of faculty workshops, the Maclellan Foundation of Chattanooga, Tennessee, granted $107,000 to cover them. The new round of workshops, scheduled for 1985–86, covered liberal arts disciplines that were not included in the NEH series. Once again Shipps, who had become academic dean at Barrington College (Rhode Island) around the time the first series was announced, and Longman, who was now the Coalition's vice president for programs, coordinated the project.[51] In fact, their capable leadership in both the NEH and Maclellan grant programs set the stage for the Coalition to become a major catalyst for Christian colleges in the area of faculty development.

Publications

As the Coalition endeavored to improve public awareness of Christ-centered higher education, publications took on an increasingly important role. As early as 1980, John Dellenback divulged that the Coalition was exploring with a publisher the production of a Christian college guide to inform prospective students and their parents about "the real uniqueness and distinctives of our kind of college."[52] The Coalition hired William B. Eerdmans Publishing Company of Grand Rapids, which was known for a distinguished line of academic and scholarly materials, to produce the guide. By late 1981 Karen Longman, who edited the handbook, informed the Coalition board of printing and distribution plans; she noted that Eerdmans was absorbing much of the advertising expense and that a Stewardship Foundation grant would aid in the distribution of the books.[53] Eerdmans actually began printing and shipping the first copies of *A Guide to Christian Colleges* at the very end of 1981. It contained useful information on each of the then sixty-three Coalition schools, as well as an introductory chapter on how a Christian liberal arts education differed from other models.[54]

The success of the *Guide* prompted Eerdmans to publish two subsequent editions, one for each of the academic years 1983–84 and 1984–85.[55] In 1987 Dellenback signed a contract with Peterson's Guides to produce a revamped handbook, *Consider a Christian College*, which was ready for release the following year. The Peterson's volume utilized research findings from a 1986 Coalition marketing project that studied the perceptions that prospective students had about Christian colleges.[56] Like the Eerdmans predecessor, the Peterson's guide went through several editions, the most recent updates published with new titles.[57] Over the years the Coalition guides have significantly boosted the visibility of Christian liberal arts institutions.

In terms of the integration of faith and learning, publishing projects emerged that were either Coalition-related or under its direct sponsorship. A good example of the former was Dean Curry's edited volume, *Evangelicals and the Bishops' Pastoral Letter*. The book stemmed from a 1983 Coalition-supported conference, "The Church and Peacemaking in the Nuclear Age," which was held in Pasadena, California. Curry, a political science professor at Messiah College, completed most of the editing while on a sabbatical with the American Studies Program during the summer of 1983.[58]

Other books resulted from cooperative arrangements between the Coalition and publishers. In one such effort, Baker Book House and ASP director John Bernbaum intended an eight-volume series of study guides to be aimed at the integration of the Bible with various academic disciplines. In 1986 Baker released the first two guides, which dealt with the issues of economic justice and employment.[59] Bernbaum, the series coordinator, envisioned that the books would help professors to incorporate Christian perspectives in the classroom and challenge students "to take the Word of God seriously in their lives."[60] One additional study guide was published in 1989.[61]

Certainly the most ambitious Coalition publishing initiative that originated in the Dellenback era was the Supplemental Textbook Series. In 1983, at the instigation of Dellenback and Karen Longman, the Coalition's board of directors authorized the Faith/Learning/Living Committee to begin investigating the feasibility of such a project.[62] The first public announcement that this series was under consideration came in early spring of 1984, after a meeting in Arlington, Virginia, at which Coalition staff met with three faculty from member institutions and one professor from a secular university. John Dellenback, who convened the meeting, commented that texts written from a faith perspective "would focus on the fundamental issues within each discipline which should be considered by thoughtful Christians."[63] Soon an editorial team was in place, headed by Nicholas Wolterstorff, then a philosophy professor at Calvin College. Mr. and Mrs. Stanley Kresge pledged funding for the first two volumes.[64]

By the end of 1985 Wolterstorff and his advisory board, including Karen Longman, had planned the textbooks for psychology, biology, literature, history, and sociology. They selected task forces for each volume, which in turn began the process of choosing authors. The Coalition also moved into the final stage of negotiations with the publisher, Harper & Row, for a minimum of eight paperback texts.[65]

Wolterstorff and the Coalition planned a conference for each volume where participants could critique drafts of manuscripts, hear presentations, attend workshops, and generally interact with colleagues. The first of these was held at Warner Pacific College (Oregon) in June 1986 for the psychology text, authored by Malcolm Jeeves of the University of St. Andrews (Scotland) and David Myers of Hope College (Michigan). Funding came from the Burlington Northern Foundation and the M. J. Murdock Charitable Trust. The conference not only aided in the editorial process, but also afforded many faculty from Coalition schools the opportunity to think more seriously about the integration of psychology and biblical faith.[66]

Before Dellenback left the Coalition presidency, similar conferences previewed the biology and literature texts.[67] In between these two gatherings, Harper released the psychology volume, the first to be published in the series.[68] Other conferences and volumes followed during the Myron Augsburger administration. Despite complaints about limited marketing, printing and binding quality, and production delays, the series provided useful classroom tools for member institutions.[69] The books also served to advance the Coalition emphasis on the integration of faith and learning; at the same time, they pointed toward a growing maturity in evangelical scholarship.

The Capital Campaign

During the Dellenback years, Coalition personnel and directors recognized that the organization needed to strengthen itself it terms of endowment funds and permanent facilities. In 1985 the development committee, then chaired by Gene Habecker, concluded that a capital campaign should be launched to ensure the Coalition's future growth and financial stability. Habecker, who was president of Huntington College, sent a memo to the board of directors in which he proposed a $2 million goal to be broken down as follows: (1) $1 million to endow the Coalition presidency; (2) $500,000 to endow the ASP; and (3) $500,000 to purchase a facility on Capitol Hill. He ended the memo with some suggestions for cultivating donors and employing a professional to oversee the campaign. The board of directors approved the committee recommendations in principle at its regular meeting in September 1985.[70]

The Coalition launched the first phase of the capital drive in 1986. In the following year, Peter Harkema of Calvin College came to Washington for six months to serve as a Coalition Fellow; part of his time was spent assisting with development efforts.[71] In the same year, the Coalition adopted a circular-shaped "C" logo and a new slogan: "For Enduring Values." The board intended for the logo and slogan "to provide national visibility and a unifying image."[72] These moves, along with some face-lifting of publications, were also designed to boost the campaign.

At the Coalition board meeting in September 1987, John Dellenback outlined various options regarding facilities in Washington, one of which was to purchase a building under construction and a nearby townhouse on Eighth Street NE, that would allow all Coalition functions in the capital to be housed at one site. After a visit to the properties, the board voted to approve their purchase "on acceptable terms and conditions contingent upon a satisfactory fund-raising plan."[73] At the end of November, the board conducted a conference call concerning the logistical aspects of the real estate contracts. Dellenback reported that the new condominium complex at 327 Eighth Street would cost $1.375 million and the adjacent townhouse at 329 Eighth Street would be $300,000, with modifications to the latter bringing the total price for both properties to $2.1 million. At that point, the Coalition had received $400,000 in campaign pledges and expected to sell DeArmond House for another $400,000. An anticipated Kresge grant and financing were projected to cover remaining costs. The board affirmed the contracts and authorized negotiations for the necessary financing.[74]

The Coalition planned to house ASP students in the new condominium and to set up staff offices in the townhouse, thus consolidating all of the organization's Washington-based activities in one place for the first time in its history. Dellenback retired before the capital campaign was completed and the new facilities were occupied. He left office, however, with the satisfaction that the Coalition would soon have a permanent home and was poised for "a significant and exciting phase of growth."[75]

Another Transition

At the Coalition's tenth anniversary meeting in 1986, board chairman Daniel Chamberlain's address looked to the future and called on the association to enhance its vitality, visibility, and viability.[76] While the Houghton president was clearly issuing a challenge concerning the years ahead, his alliteration in many ways could be used to summarize the achievements of the Dellenback decade. Under the former congressman's leadership, which was backed by excellent support from staff and constituents, the Coalition undeniably became more vital, visible, and viable. In addition to the programs and accomplishments already discussed, the Coalition established a faculty exchange program, a January term student exchange program, a tuition waiver exchange agreement, conferences and meetings for various categories of college administrators, and overseas study tours for professors and administrators. The multitude of Coalition activities was supported by a budget that reached $800,000 in Dellenback's last full year.[77]

Through all that transpired, a movement for Christ-centered higher education emerged, one that was not dependent on any particular individual. Rather, the movement consisted of many players, programs, and networks that ensured some continuity when leadership changed, as it did when Dellenback stepped down from the Coalition presidency early in 1988.[78]

FIVE

Prophetic
and Global Impulses

~~~~~

Myron Augsburger

When John Dellenback told the Coalition's board of directors in 1987 that he planned to retire in 1988, a search committee chaired by Clyde Cook, president of Biola University, began screening potential presidential candidates. The committee ultimately asked Myron Augsburger in the fall of 1987 to consider accepting the position. At the time, Augsburger was on his way to India, so he told the committee that he would pray about the offer. By early 1988 he responded affirmatively; at the Coalition meeting of school presidents in early February, he was presented as the board's unanimous choice to succeed Dellenback. For this occasion, Augsburger's wife Esther, who was an artist, prepared a sculpture in honor of the Dellenbacks. Meanwhile, the board of directors projected the transition in leadership for late spring or early summer.[1]

Augsburger was a well-known figure in both the evangelical world and Christian higher education. The Mennonite preacher, educator, and theologian earned two bachelor's degrees from Eastern Mennonite College, a Master of Divinity degree from Goshen Biblical Seminary, and Master of Theology and Doctor of Theology degrees from Union Theological Seminary in Richmond, Virginia. He served from 1965 to

1980 as president and professor of theology at Eastern Mennonite College and Seminary. During his period of leadership at the Harrisonburg, Virginia, institution he participated in the founding of both the Christian College Consortium in 1971 and the Coalition in 1976. In 1981 he became the first pastor of Washington Community Fellowship, a new multidenominational church on Capitol Hill that soon attracted American Studies Program staff and developed a ministry to ASP students and alumni. In addition to his pastoral duties, he conducted evangelistic campaigns with Inter-Church Crusades and sat on the Coalition's board of reference.[2] While Augsburger certainly did not have Dellenback's political connections, his experience in higher education was much more extensive.

Since Augsburger assumed the Coalition presidency in a half-time capacity, he remained for a while on the church staff as Minister of the Word.[3] Coalition staff increasingly shouldered the administrative load in various areas; they viewed Augsburger as a visionary who did not seem as interested in operational details. In fact, staff typically characterized his management style as "hands-off."[4]

Augsburger contributed most significantly as an educator through Coalition seminars and conferences that focused on education from a Christian worldview. His earlier curricular innovations with an interdisciplinary studies program at Eastern Mennonite helped him to hone his expertise in this area. His theological training and many writings also served him well as he challenged the member colleges to integrate biblical faith with learning.[5]

In addition, Augsburger articulated a mission for the organization, a task that suited his obvious oratorical gifts. In many ways, he shared Nicholas Wolterstorff's desire that Christian colleges move into a new stage of development where they would nurture a special focus on "the Christian in society."[6] Of course, Wolterstorff's Reformed understanding differed from Augsburger's Anabaptist vision, but they embraced some of the same priorities. For example, Augsburger's stated goals for the Coalition and for Christian colleges in general often echoed Wolterstorff's concerns. At the time that his appointment was announced, Augsburger pointed to the need for curricular materials that would grapple with "human rights and justice issues"; he also spoke forcefully of moving beyond American parochialism "to help our nation find a place of compassion in the global community."[7] Toward the end of his presidency, he delivered an address at a Coalition annual meet-

A reception honoring President and Mrs. John Dellenback. From left to right: Jeanie Herbert, Mary Jane Dellenback, and Dr. John Dellenback.

In 1975 Dr. Gordon Werkema was president of the Christian College Consortium, a smaller sister organization still in existence, when he proposed "a new organization . . . to be known as the Council of or for Christian Colleges." Little did he know what would come of that proposal!

Before acquiring property on Eighth Street NE, the American Studies Program staff were housed in the DeArmond House at 14 Fourth Street NE. It then served as the CCCU president's home from 1989–94. Pictured are the ASP/CCCU staff and spouses circa 1986.

A ceremony during the "changing of the guard" at the 1989 Annual Presidents' Conference. From left to right: Dr. Myron Augsburger, incoming CCCU president; Dr. Clyde Cook, president of Biola University; Mary Jane Dellenback; and Dr. John Dellenback, outgoing CCCU president.

The 1989 Annual Presidents' Conference. Dr. John Dellenback greeting Mrs. Gloria Gaither, then a member of the board of reference and later on the board of directors, 1994–2000.

Reconstruction in 1990 of the CCCU's headquarters office building on Eighth Street NE, Washington, D.C.

Board chairman Bud Austin presents a gift to outgoing CCCU president Dr. Myron Augsburger and his wife Esther.

A group at the 1990 dedication of The Dellenback Center, the building that houses students attending the American Studies Program. The three men in the middle are, from left to right: Dr. Richard C. Halverson, former chaplain of the Senate and later the first CCCU Distinguished Senior Fellow; Dr. Myron Augsburger, president; and Dr. John Dellenback, former president.

First Student Program Directors Retreat in 1994 hosted by Rich Gathro and Ruth Melkonian. Back row (left to right): Anthony Chamberlain, Latin American Studies Program; Ruth Melkonian, CCCU Program Associate; Rich Gathro, CCCU Vice President for Student Programs; Marilyn and Dr. Cliff Gardner, Middle East Studies Program. Front row (left to right): Jeannie and Dr. Jerry Herbert, American Studies Program; Doug and Fran Briggs, Los Angeles Film Studies Center; Dr. Harley Wagler, Russian Studies Program.

Three leaders chat at the 1999 Annual Presidents' Conference. From left to right: Dr. John Corts, executive director of the Billy Graham Evangelical Association, after accepting the Mark O. Hatfield Award on behalf of Billy Graham; Missouri Congressman Roy Blunt, conference speaker and former president of Southwest Baptist University; and Dr. Paul Corts, brother of John Corts, a CCCU board member and president of Palm Beach Atlantic College.

President Bob Andringa (center) greets two Missouri political leaders. On the left is Congressman Roy Blunt and on the right is Senator John Ashcroft who spoke to the presidents and guests at the 1999 Annual Presidents' Conference.

President Bob Andringa having fun during a presentation to Dr. James Bultman, then CCCU board chairman and president of Northwestern College (Iowa).

During the 1999 Annual Presidents' Conference, Jay Kesler, president of Taylor University, pays tribute to Rev. Billy Graham, recipient of the Mark O. Hatfield Leadership Award.

Coalition for
Christian Colleges
& Universities

Dr. Royce Money (left), president of Abilene Christian University and later CCCU board chairman, enjoys a moment with Senator Mark O. Hatfield, longtime friend of Christian higher education.

Charles Colson (left), named the second CCCU Distinguished Senior Fellow, was the speaker during the 1997 Annual Presidents' Conference. Here he is talking with CCCU president Bob Andringa.

President Bob Andringa presenting his report at the 1996 annual meeting.

Four great leaders in our history at the Annual Presidents' Conference in 1989. From left to right: Dr. Myron Augsburger, president; Mr. Ken Wesner, then chairman of the ServiceMaster Corporation; Dr. John Dellenback, CCCU president emeritus; and Senator Mark O. Hatfield.

The 1994 Annual Presidents' Conference. From left to right: Dr. Myron Augsburger, CCCU president; Dr. Bud Austin, president of LeTourneau University and CCCU board chairman; and Dr. John Bernbaum, then the vice president and director of the CCCU's Russian Initiative.

In 1998 Dr. Arthur Holmes, professor emeritus of Wheaton College, was the first recipient of the Mark O. Hatfield Leadership Award.

Planning meeting at the Centre for Medieval and Renaissance Studies for the Honours Programme at Oxford and the Templeton Project. Left to right: Kathy and Rich Gathro, Vice President for Student Programs; Dr. John Feneley, principal of CMRS; Dr. Karen Longman, Vice President for Professional Development and Research; and Dr. Shirley Thomas, John Brown University.

Three students attending the Latin American Studies Program in Costa Rica, shown here in front of the building owned by the Council.

The board of directors of Christian University GlobalNet, a supporting organization to the Council formed in 1998, at a recent meeting in Denver. From left to right: Dr. Bob Andringa, ex officio; Dr. Michael Zastrocky, The Gartner Group; Dr. David Gyertson, president, Taylor University; Evan Morgan, president and CEO of CUGN; and Dr. Jud Carlberg, board chairman and president of Gordon College. Board member Loren Gresham, president of Southern Nazarene University, was not present at this meeting.

The newest of the Council's three buildings on Capitol Hill is this 8000-square-foot structure completed in late 1999. It houses several staff, a large conference room with teleconference capacity, a small conference room, two guest suites, and a fitness center for ASP students and staff. *(Photo courtesy of VOA Associates, Inc. and Maxwell MacKenzie, photographer.)*

The welcome center in the new headquarters building. *(Photo courtesy of VOA Associates, Inc. and Maxwell MacKenzie, photographer.)*

ing on "Our Mission in Higher Education," in which he spelled out the social and cultural task of Christian schools:

> Christian colleges should act in society as agents of social justice. The Christian liberal arts college does not combat racism, sexism, materialism and violence by the singular message of the gospel alone, but by the breadth of cultural values of equity, love and justice as they are enriched by Christian dialogue.[8]

In short, Augsburger positioned himself as the prophet of a servant organization. His commitments to peace, social justice, and a global vision influenced both the continuing Coalition programs as well as new initiatives that were inaugurated between 1988 and 1994. Some in the Coalition questioned the direction of the Augsburger agenda, citing in particular the pacifist orientation of the ASP during his presidency.[9]

The former Eastern Mennonite president also raised some eyebrows with his critique of evangelicalism, which he presented at the Coalition's annual meeting in 1994. Although both the Consortium and the Coalition had been products of the post-fundamentalist, new evangelical resurgence following World War II, Augsburger argued that the movement had become a "sub-culture" or an "ethnicity" that exhibited some serious limitations. He specifically mentioned individualism, pietism, privatism, nationalism, inerrancy of word (versus inerrancy of meaning), a Greek view of personality, and Aristotelianism as the besetting sins of many American evangelicals.[10] Augsburger clearly saw himself as an evangelical, yet as a socially conscious Mennonite he often found himself swimming against prevailing evangelical currents.

Augsburger's priorities differed from those of his predecessor in two major ways. First, despite his many calls for social integrity and justice, Augsburger's Anabaptist roots militated against an aggressive involvement in lobbying and public policy endeavors in the nation's capital.[11] These items did not suddenly disappear from the Coalition's list of purposes. Indeed, Augsburger occasionally met with White House staff and members of Congress. The organization also continued to set forth positions on issues like religious liberty and academic freedom in the District of Columbia, student access to government aid, and the right of member institutions to hire only committed Christians. In regard to political and legal matters, however, Rich Gathro and the Coalition's Government Relations Committee generally took the lead. The committee also worked cooperatively with the National Association of Independent Colleges and Universities and the Association of Christian Schools International to help protect the interests of Coalition members in Washington.[12]

Second, whereas Dellenback pushed vigorously to enlarge the Coalition's membership, Augsburger was content to let it grow at a much slower pace. With the "critical mass" apparently in place, the new president concentrated on clarifying the expectations and strengthening the relationships of member institutions. Only eleven schools that are still regular members of the CCCU today joined during the Augsburger era. In keeping with past trends, new members once again magnified the Coalition's denominational diversity. They represented the following traditions: General Conference Mennonite (Bluffton), Southern Baptist (California Baptist, Oklahoma Baptist, and Union), General Association of Regular Baptist (Cedarville and Grand Rapids Baptist, which has since been renamed Cornerstone University), Independent Baptist (Western Baptist), Associate Reformed Presbyterian (Erskine), Presbyterian (Montreat), Christian Church/Churches of Christ (Pacific Christian, which was later renamed Hope International University), and Assemblies of God (Northwest College).[13] In light of Augsburger's concerns about some features of evangelicalism, it is interesting that most of the new members would have been classified as conservative evangelical or, in a few cases, fundamentalist. In fact, unlike the Consortium, which drew distinct lines between evangelicals and fundamentalists, the Coalition welcomed fundamentalist institutions that met membership standards.

During the Augsburger presidency, the Coalition addressed proposed revisions in membership criteria. In response to concerns about some applicants, the board approved a new guideline in the area of financial responsibility. Likewise, the association attempted to define more precisely what it meant for a college or university to have a primary orientation in the liberal arts and sciences. The board decided to require that new members offer at least one major in each of the following categories: fine arts/humanities; social/behavioral sciences; and natural/mathematical sciences.[14] Finally, Augsburger suggested a new category of "associate" member for institutions that did not qualify for full membership. He drew up criteria but the concept was not actually accepted by the board and implemented until the Andringa presidency.[15] Overall, slower growth under Augsburger allowed the

Coalition to refine membership standards and to consolidate itself as a movement.

Myron Augsburger unmistakably brought a different set of gifts, perspectives, and interests to the Coalition presidency than did John Dellenback. Moreover, the former's prophetic bent often stood in stark contrast to the latter's more pragmatic approach. Both leaders, however, advocated the cause of Christ-centered higher education with ability and enthusiasm. Furthermore, Augsburger inherited some initiatives from his predecessor that sometimes required as much time and energy as newer projects.

The Capital Campaign Continues

When Augsburger became Coalition president in 1988, the capital campaign that began in 1986 was still in its early stages. Although one of the original goals of the drive had been endowment support, the purchase and development of the Eighth Street properties quickly overshadowed it. While longtime staffer Rich Gathro continued to work on logistical matters related to the new buildings, Augsburger hired Nancy Goodrich as director of development to help with fundraising. The wife of a D.C. Superior Court judge, Goodrich brought experience in education, business, and community service to her Coalition post. She worked at the Coalition for two years, during which the capital campaign was in its busiest phase; she and Augsburger spent countless hours soliciting potential donors.[16]

Developments in the fall of 1988 gave the campaign a boost in momentum. First, forty ASP students moved into the Coalition's new four-story condominium on Eighth Street, thus providing the ASP with a permanent base for the first time. Second, the Coalition named Kenneth Wessner, chairman of the board of the ServiceMaster Company, and Senator Mark Hatfield as cochairs of what was now a $2.8 million National Capital Campaign.[17] Third, the Kresge Foundation awarded a $300,000 challenge grant to the drive, contingent on the Coalition raising another $1.8 million by the beginning of 1990.[18] Other major gifts in 1988 came from the Fred B. Meyer Charitable Trust, the Maclellan Foundation, and the ServiceMaster Company.[19] The announcement of these grants, along with the occupation of the new ASP condominiums and the stature of the cochairs, lent visibility and credibility to the campaign.

At the Coalition's annual meeting early in 1989, the board of directors voted to name the new facilities on Eighth Street The Dellenback Center, in honor of President Emeritus Dellenback and his wife Mary Jane. The Coalition also indicated that the halfway mark had been reached in what was now a $3 million fund drive. Most of the increase from earlier projections reflected additional renovation costs for the townhouse next to the condominium.[20]

By the end of 1989 the National Capital Campaign had raised over $2.8 million. Once again, foundation and corporate gifts constituted a major portion of the funds. Contributors included the Stewardship Foundation, the Stratford Foundation, the M. J. Murdock Charitable Trust, the Merillat Foundation, and Herman Miller. The Coalition's member schools and interested individuals also donated to the cause.[21]

As the campaign neared its completion in early 1990, the Coalition board agreed to purchase additional buildings at 321 and 323 Eighth Street NE, for $385,000. The board and staff projected the extra properties for future use as offices and planned to rent them to other parties for a period of four or five years.[22] These acquisitions gave the Coalition a sizable stretch of property between 321 and 329 Eighth Street NE.

In March of 1990 Coalition staff moved into the newly-renovated townhouse next to The Dellenback Center. A time of celebration occurred the following month when The Dellenback Center was officially dedicated. Richard Halverson, U.S. Senate chaplain, gave the keynote address for the festive occasion.[23] This event essentially marked both the end of a successful National Capital Campaign and the beginning of Coalition history at a new, unified location. It also served as a suitable tribute to the tireless efforts of those who guided the campaign.

Publications Expand

The completion of the capital campaign was not the only accomplishment of the Augsburger presidency. The Coalition's Supplemental Textbook Series, published by HarperCollins, witnessed its most productive period during this time. Karen Longman, a Coalition vice president, and Nicholas Wolterstorff, who left Calvin for Yale, continued to coordinate the task forces, national conferences, and publication schedules. Between 1989 and 1993 volumes were released for literature, biology, history, business, sociology, and music. Several

Coalition colleges were represented among the authors, including Calvin, Eastern, Gordon, Goshen, and Wheaton.[24] The supplemental texts gained even wider circulation through special publishing arrangements with InterVarsity Press–England and InterVarsity Press–Korea, as well as the release of some volumes in Danish, Dutch, French, and Russian.[25] The series still stands as one of the CCCU's significant achievements in promoting the integration of faith and learning.

Established Programs Flourish

During the Augsburger era, the Coalition maintained further continuity with the Dellenback presidency through the American Studies Program, the Latin American Studies Program, and faculty development workshops. At the same time, these already functioning projects experienced some changes. In the ASP, which admitted its one thousandth student in the fall of 1988, staff adjustments became necessary as veteran ASP personnel Rich Gathro and John Bernbaum assumed other Coalition responsibilities. In the fall of 1989 Gathro moved to part-time status as Augsburger's executive assistant so he could serve as interim pastor at his church. When he returned to full-time capacity in 1990, it was as vice president for advancement. Then in 1991 he became vice president for operations. Bernbaum relinquished the ASP directorship at the end of 1991 because of his duties as executive vice president and director of the Russian Initiative, and Jerry Herbert took over as head of the ASP.[26] By that time the ASP had observed fifteen years of continuous operation in the nation's capital.

Gathro's transition toward more administrative assignments opened the door for Steven Garber to join the ASP faculty on a part-time basis in 1989. Garber, who earned a Ph.D. in higher education at Penn State, earlier worked with InterVarsity staff at the University of Kansas and with the Coalition for Christian Outreach in the Pittsburgh area. He came to the ASP with a real burden for worldview issues; as a result, he took a leading role in an ASP curriculum revision by introducing a "Foundations for Public Involvement" course. Garber designed this to help students develop a theological and philosophical framework for dealing with public policy issues. His concern that students relate faith to their lives in the world eventually led him to write *The Fabric of Faithfulness*, a book which aptly reflected the Coalition's long-term interest in the integration of faith, learning, and living. Today Garber serves the CCCU as a scholar-in-residence.[27]

The Latin American Studies Program likewise saw some personnel changes. Roland Hoksbergen, the first director of the program, left at the end of the 1988–89 academic year and returned to Calvin College. By that time, the LASP had enrolled around one hundred students, many of whom reported on the life-changing nature of their experiences in another culture.[28] In the spring of 1989 the Coalition's Student Academic Programs Committee announced the appointment of Christopher Dearnley as Hoksbergen's successor. A graduate of Wheaton and the Harvard Graduate School of Business Administration, Dearnley previously worked in Costa Rica as an economic development consultant.[29] When Dearnley resigned his post at the end of the 1989–90 academic year, he was replaced by Anthony Chamberlain, a Messiah alumnus and Ph.D. candidate at the University of Maryland, who came to the position with cross-cultural experience in China and South America. Anthony, the son of Houghton president Daniel Chamberlain, has over the past decade helped the LASP procure permanent facilities, has introduced academic concentrations in tropical science and international business, and has effectively overseen a vibrant program.[30]

Finally, faculty development workshops and seminars aimed at promoting academic excellence continued to flourish during the Augsburger presidency. Beyond the supplemental textbook conferences, the Coalition maintained a full slate of discipline-specific and interdisciplinary workshops designed to stimulate faculty thinking about the integration of Christianity with teaching and scholarship. Karen Longman still held primary responsibility for faculty development, and the M. J. Murdock Charitable Trust continued to be a major funding source.[31] Innovations included the first workshop designed specifically for new professors in 1990 and the first regional faculty workshop in 1993, which addressed the topic "The Use of Scripture in Teaching the Liberal Arts." The new faculty sessions brought together Stanley Gaede, then of Gordon College; Harold Heie, then of Messiah College; and Arthur Holmes of Wheaton College. These three have continued to mentor younger faculty in similar settings over the past decade.[32]

Augsburger wisely allowed the Coalition to sustain strong programs with an established track record. He likewise depended on the expertise of his staff to ensure that the ASP, LASP, and faculty development efforts functioned at levels consistent with their reputations. At the same time, the Coalition president did not shrink from encouraging and helping to implement new endeavors, especially when they meshed with his prophetic and global concerns.

New Programs and Initiatives

Early in his presidency, Myron Augsburger dreamed of the Coalition sponsoring a series of "think tanks" that would engage Christians in meaningful dialogue about important social and theological issues. As early as 1988 he reported to the board of directors about the possibility of holding an institute on reconciliation and evangelism at the University of Zurich in Switzerland.[33] In 1990 the think tank idea reached fruition as twenty-eight people from eight countries, calling themselves the Zurich Fellowship, met in the Swiss city to address problems relating to environmental stewardship, international relations, economic development, and education. Augsburger, who convened the meeting under Coalition auspices, proclaimed that one of its goals "was to provide the international community with an alternative model for decision-making."[34] While Augsburger apparently intended for the Zurich Fellowship to be an ongoing project, no follow-up sessions were held in Switzerland.

Back in the United States, the Coalition sponsored several more think tanks with a more modest agenda than the Zurich gathering. Between 1991 and 1993, various administrators and faculty from member schools came together for interdisciplinary discussions with key Christian leaders and thinkers, including ethicist Stanley Hauerwas, missiologist Lesslie Newbigin, theologian Carl Henry, and cultural critic Os Guinness. A final think tank held in 1994 aimed at a multicultural dialogue on the topic "Developing a Theology of Inclusion."[35] While the term *think tank* may have been misleading, the conferences provided participants with useful guidance for applying the Christian faith to the social order.

Another new initiative that enhanced the Coalition's service role actually had its roots in a 1987 study of how Christian colleges were developing their resources. Wesley Willmer, then the director of development at Wheaton College, compiled the report under the title *Friends, Funds and Freshmen for Christian Colleges*.[36] Willmer's work sparked a $30,000 grant from the Lilly Endowment in the spring of 1989; the

71

Coalition utilized this money for a planning/feasibility study that assessed the fundraising effectiveness of member institutions.[37] Willmer, who had moved to an advancement position at Biola University, directed the new project, which resulted in a second edition of his earlier book and a proposal to Lilly for a much larger grant.[38]

Late in 1990, Lilly awarded the Coalition a $510,000 grant for a three-year project on "Increasing Fundraising Effectiveness." The Coalition named Rebekah Basinger, former executive assistant to the president at Messiah College, as project director.[39] She coordinated several workshops for presidents, development officers, trustees, academic deans, and female fundraisers from Coalition colleges. She also published a newsletter, *DevelopLink*, and arranged for development office audits at member schools. By the time the project ended in 1994, all Coalition institutions had participated in at least one activity funded by the grant and one-third had requested development office audits.[40] Since Christian colleges typically do not enjoy large endowments and often struggle valiantly to balance their budgets, it is not surprising that they so readily took advantage of the Lilly Project opportunities.

Augsburger's passion for social justice led to a new initiative on racial diversity. Early in 1989 he proposed to the board of directors that minority education should be the Coalition's highest priority. With funding from Pew Charitable Trusts, the Coalition brought the Minority Concerns Task Force together in Philadelphia in the spring of 1990, where participants urged the creation of a national resource office for minorities.[41]

Two developments late in 1991 showed Augsburger's readiness to move forward on the diversity theme. First, the Coalition helped to bring ethnic and minority issues into sharper focus by co-publishing a volume of collected essays on the subject. The contributors suggested that, for the most part, Coalition schools failed to mirror the ethnic diversity of the surrounding culture.[42] Second, soon after the book's release, the Coalition announced the appointment of Deborah Bailey as director of a new venture, the Minority Concerns Project. A doctoral candidate in higher education at the University of Maryland, Bailey previously directed the Washington Center's Minority Leaders Fellowship Program.[43]

During her two and one-half years heading the Office of Racial/Ethnic Diversity (ORED), Bailey was assisted by Calvin graduate Rhonda Roorda. She worked hard to raise the consciousness levels on Coalition campuses, and to facilitate the networking of minority faculty and students. Significant funding for the program came from the fourteen Coalition colleges that served as model sites for implementing ORED strategies. Through Bailey's office, the Coalition either organized or co-sponsored several conferences and workshops, some of which were underwritten by the M. J. Murdock Charitable Trust. A quarterly newsletter, *The Open Door*, reported on the project's progress and also provided information on various campus initiatives.[44]

By 1994, when Augsburger's departure from the Coalition was imminent, the diversity project had generated controversy on some campuses and among board members. Furthermore, it was operating at a deficit and external funding was set to expire. Much to Augsburger's regret, the ORED was closed in the summer of 1994; later, under president Bob Andringa, the Coalition would aim for racial and ethnic inclusiveness in a more decentralized fashion.[45]

One of the new student programs that emerged during the Augsburger era was originally conceived in the Christian College Consortium. In 1989 a Consortium task force completed a feasibility study for a proposed Film Production Studies Program to be patterned after the Coalition's ASP and LASP. An anonymous donor funded the task force and also stood ready to support an ongoing program in Hollywood. Early on in the planning, the Consortium sought to involve the Coalition; Myron Augsburger and John Bernbaum were in consultation with interested persons, and Karen Longman served on the task force as an ex officio member.[46]

Since the Consortium expected to develop the film studies project and then turn it over to the Coalition, Bernbaum proposed to Augsburger that "some fundamental decisions need to be made about future relationships" between the two organizations. He also alluded to earlier hard feelings about "ownership" of the ASP as a potential obstacle to cooperation.[47] During a subsequent Coalition board meeting where the directors discussed the Consortium/Coalition issue at length, Augsburger and Roberta Hestenes of Eastern College even suggested unification of the two groups as an option.[48]

Although the two organizations made no serious effort to merge, they reached an amicable agreement on the new program. This step was expedited by the donor's willingness to direct her grant to the Coalition.[49] By late 1989 the Coalition's Student Academic Programs Committee recommended and the board of directors approved, by telephone vote, that the Consortium feasibility study be accepted and that the Coalition inaugurate the Los Angeles Film Studies Center (LAFSC). The Coalition assigned John Bernbaum to guide the project on a half-time basis for several months.[50]

In 1990 the Coalition appointed Douglas Briggs as LAFSC director and he began work in July. Briggs came to the new post from Bethel College in Minnesota, where he taught theatre and served at various times in administrative offices. Prior to his stint at Bethel, he taught theatre at San Francisco State, where he earned B.A. and M.A. degrees, and also at California State in Fresno and Northwestern College in Minnesota.[51]

The LAFSC opened its first semester in January of 1991 at rented facilities in Burbank. The inaugural group of eight students took three courses: "Inside Hollywood: The Work and Workings of the Film Industry"; "Keeping Conscience: Ethical Challenges in the Entertainment Industry"; and "Film in Culture: Exploring a Christian Perspective on the Nature and Influence of Film." They also benefited from internships in the film and television industries.[52] Following the lead of the ASP and LASP, the LAFSC curriculum purposefully aimed to integrate faith, learning, and living.

Under Briggs's creative leadership, the LAFSC gradually established a presence in what some viewed as a hostile environment. Interns came to be respected and sought after by several film production offices. Further, the LAFSC launched a graduate scholarship program to help support a long-range mission, which Briggs described as developing "a cadre of Christian men and women who desire to move into the mainstream Hollywood entertainment business, bringing with them a commitment to the enhancement of Judeo-Christian values in their life and work."[53] Briggs continues to lead this innovative program today from an industry office building near Burbank.[54]

Clearly the Augsburger years saw a remarkable surge in Coalition program development. Three additional cooperative efforts illustrated the Coalition's varied agenda: (1) the Harvey Fellows Program of graduate scholarships, initiated in 1991 with the financial backing of the Mustard Seed Foundation; (2) a joint project with the Center for Public Justice to study urban poverty, launched in 1992 with funding from Pew Charitable Trusts; and (3) a 1993 women's conference on gender issues in higher education, co-sponsored with Eastern College.[55] At the same time, the Coalition pursued some exciting international opportunities that dovetailed quite well with some of Augsburger's basic concerns.

Additional Global Connections[56]

The stunning collapse of the Soviet empire in 1989 opened many new doors for Christian ministry in Eastern Europe. In response to the major political changes that ensued, the Coalition convened a meeting of parachurch groups and nine member colleges late in 1989 to discuss the possible consequences for Christian higher education. By early 1990 the Coalition announced its Soviet Initiatives Project, for which John Bernbaum took primary responsibility. In March of that year Karen Longman visited Moscow and Leningrad, where she met with educators, government officials, and Christian leaders to investigate the possibility of partnership agreements between Coalition schools and Soviet universities.[57]

In September of 1990 sixteen Soviet academicians, including government agency heads and administrators from universities and technical institutes, spent ten days in the United States learning about American higher education. They visited the Coalition offices in Washington and the campuses of three Coalition colleges, Messiah, Eastern, and Eastern Mennonite. After a series of consultations, the Soviet delegation and the Coalition representatives signed a Protocol of Intentions, which called for cooperation in several educational areas.[58]

As a follow-up to the Protocol, Bernbaum led a Coalition group to the Soviet Union in October. Before leaving, the Coalition vice president assessed the rapidly unfolding situation:

> This is truly one of those rare "moments of truth" in a nation's history when basic decisions are being made that will set the future course for millions of people. Our desire is to be witnesses of Jesus Christ to our Soviet friends and to help them restructure their educational system so that moral and spiritual values are integrated into all facets of their academic programs. The roots of Russian spirituality lie deep in their collective history and must be rediscovered. We also hope to challenge our own students to gain a vision for their lives that might include building bridges between our two cultures.[59]

Thus undergirded by a strong sense of mission, Bernbaum's delegation laid the groundwork for several student and faculty exchanges, as well as for other endeavors in the formerly Communist nation.[60] For example, Augsburger and four American professors journeyed to Moscow in the spring of 1992 to lecture at some of the city's universities.[61]

The Soviet project, eventually renamed the Russian Initiative, became one of the Coalition's most dynamic programs with eighteen member schools signing on as partners. James Engel of Eastern College and Bernbaum facilitated the development of a values-based Master of Business Administration degree curriculum for use in Russian universities; course modules were written by Russian and American professors working as a team. The Coalition reported on this and other ventures in a special newsletter, *Russia Link*.[62]

As the Russian Initiative gained momentum, Bernbaum proposed in 1992 that the Coalition begin a Russian Studies Program (RSP) similar to the one in Latin America. The Coalition board subsequently approved the idea, and Harley Wagler was announced in the summer of 1993 as the director. Wagler, who studied Slavic languages and literatures in graduate programs at the University of Kansas, had lived and taught for over twelve years in the former Soviet Union and other parts of Eastern Europe. The RSP's first semester commenced in January of 1994. The curriculum called for students to spend the first two weeks in Moscow, then study Russian language, culture, and history for ten weeks in Nizhni Novgorod; the final three weeks involved internships and service projects in St. Petersburg. Wagler continues to lead this program from its base in Nizhni Novgorod.[63]

One other outgrowth of the Russian Initiative ultimately took Bernbaum away from the Coalition. Early on in the project, the Russian State Committee on Science and Higher Education approached Augsburger and Bernbaum about starting a Christian liberal arts college or institute in Moscow. In 1993 Bernbaum convened a meeting at Wheaton College to discuss with Christian leaders and educators the possibility of launching a Russian-American Christian University. Later in the same year, Augsburger and Bernbaum traveled to Moscow for further planning sessions, which included Russian government officials. The following year Augsburger assigned Bernbaum to full-time status on the Russian Initiative. The board supported Augsburger in this appointment and tentatively expressed its support for the university as "one facet" of the Russian project. By 1995, during the Andringa presidency, the board raised questions about the compatibility of the university plan with the Coalition's mission statement. Bernbaum, sensing a call to devote his full attention to the university, left the Coalition after almost twenty years of service. The Russian-American Christian University became an affiliate member of the CCCU in 1997.[64] Needless to say, Bernbaum's vision and energy accounted for much of the Russian Initiative's success. In recognition of his pioneering educational efforts in Russia, the University of Nizhni Novgorod awarded its first honorary doctorate to Bernbaum in 1995.[65]

Another international endeavor, which was started in 1991, provided summer study opportunities for Coalition college students in England. Augsburger arranged a cooperative program with the Centre for Medieval & Renaissance Studies at Oxford, which is affiliated with Keble College and Wycliffe Hall. Designed with a primary emphasis on the Reformation and Renaissance, the Oxford summer sessions have combined lectures by university dons, interdisciplinary seminars, tutorials, and field trips to historic sites. Although the board raised some concerns after the first summer about the Oxford professors' abilities to integrate faith with their teaching, the program has continued to provide stimulating learning experiences for Coalition students and faculty who sometimes accompany them.[66]

Finally, the Middle East Studies Program (MESP) represented yet another overseas initiative by the Coalition. It resulted from four years of discussion and planning; in particular, a Murdock-funded summer faculty workshop in 1991—"The Muslim World in the Christian College Classroom"—helped to spark a feasibility study and definitive proposal. In 1992 the Student Academic Programs Committee and the board of directors approved the MESP. In early 1993 Karen Longman and Ronald Mahurin, then a professor at Gordon College, traveled to Cairo, Egypt, to plan for the opening of the program. Clifford Gardner, who was formerly at the American University of Cairo, was brought to Washington for board interviews and was named as the first director. In September of 1993 fourteen students flew with Gardner to Cairo for the MESP's inaugural semester. The curriculum included such courses as "Introduction to Arabic," "Peoples and Cultures of the Middle East," "Islam in the Modern World," and "Conflict and Change in the Middle East Today." Students also engaged in service projects and spent two weeks of the semester in Israel. Richard Cahill, previously a history professor at Westmont College, has guided the MESP since 1996.[67] While obviously part of the Coalition's emphasis on globalization during Augsburger's presidency, the MESP demonstrates once again the enduring influence of the American Studies Program curricular model.

Another Leadership Change

Myron Augsburger announced in September of 1993 that he would end his leadership of the Coalition effective June 30, 1994, to pursue other ministries in teaching, writing, and evangelism.[68] His six-year presidency coincided with an explosion of new programs and initiatives, many of which reflected his interests in social justice and global engagement. At a time when some like sociologist James Davison Hunter questioned whether Christian colleges undermined theological orthodoxy, Augsburger eloquently affirmed the integrity of Christ-centered higher education both in Washington and on scores of Coalition campuses.[69] Aided by a creative, resourceful, and dedicated staff, he oversaw a growing enterprise with a plethora of activities that testified to its institutional vibrancy. In his last fiscal year as president, the Coalition reported total revenues of $3.3 million and net assets of $2.5 million.[70]

The Coalition, however, was poised to enter a new phase that called for special administrative and organizational skills. Several board members apparently desired more focused, full-time leadership that would also be more engaged in the Washington political scene.[71] In due time, the mantle passed from a visionary prophet and educator to a more practical chief executive officer.

SIX

The Maturing of a Professional Association

Robert Andringa

After Myron Augsburger indicated his intention to relinquish the Coalition presidency, board chairman Alvin "Bud" Austin, president of LeTourneau University, began organizing a search committee. The committee, which Austin chaired, engaged David McKenna as a consultant and advertised nationally to help identify promising candidates. Late in 1993, Austin called Bob Andringa in Denver to inquire about his possible interest in the position. Andringa, who previously had done a presidential assessment for Austin at LeTourneau, enjoyed the Denver area and his consulting work that was based there; hence, his initial response was less than enthusiastic. At the suggestion of his wife Sue, however, they prayed about it for several days. After about two weeks, he sensed that heading the Coalition was a divine call and that he ought to accept it. Thus, at its annual meeting early in 1994, the Coalition announced Andringa's appointment as Augsburger's successor, effective July 1.[1]

Andringa's impressive résumé pointed to his political savvy, awareness of basic issues in higher education, and broad experience in executive leadership. The recipient of three degrees from Michigan State

University, including a Ph.D. in higher education, he first entered the political realm in the nation's capital in 1969. Congressman Albert Quie, a Republican from Minnesota, appointed Andringa as minority staff director for the House Committee on Education and Labor. During the seven years that he spent at that post, the future Coalition president gained a reputation for expertise in education policy development. For example, he helped to shape legislation like the Higher Education Amendments of 1972.[2] Coincidentally, his service on the House committee led to a working relationship with Congressman John Dellenback, who was the ranking minority member of a subcommittee on postsecondary education.[3]

In 1978 Quie ran for governor of Minnesota. After Andringa had managed the successful campaign, Quie appointed him as senior policy advisor. Then in 1980 the Andringas moved west to Denver, where Bob served as executive director for the Education Commission of the States. After five years with this agency, he founded The Andringa Group, a consulting and professional service firm committed to aiding nonprofit institutions (including Coalition colleges) in board development, strategic planning, and presidential searches. In 1992 he established CEO Dialogues, a nonprofit ministry aimed especially at assisting leaders of Christian organizations. Even as Coalition/CCCU president he has continued to consult with boards.[4]

Andringa's spiritual pilgrimage intersected with his educational and professional development. At Michigan State, he came to faith in Christ through the ministry of Campus Crusade. In Washington, his first contact with Congressman Quie was through the National Prayer Breakfast movement. Then his career as a consultant connected him with additional parachurch organizations such as Young Life. In fact, The Andringa Group was based in a region of the country to which many parachurch agencies were relocating. Since the Coalition encompassed schools from a wide variety of Protestant traditions, Andringa's transdenominational, broadly evangelical background surely was viewed as a plus. As president, he has played down denominational differences and encouraged unity in the essentials of the faith as the best way of keeping the association focused on the cause of Christ-centered higher education.[5]

Soon after taking the helm as the Coalition's full-time CEO, Andringa turned his attention to structural matters involving the staff and the board of directors. In response to what he perceived as an ad hoc and unwieldy staff operation, he tightened procedures and clarified responsibilities in several ways. Since John Bernbaum was now full time with the Russian Initiative, Andringa placed all student programs under vice president Rich Gathro, and all professional development and research activities under vice president Karen Longman. Kyle Royer, who had been serving as accountant and business manager since 1989, became vice president for finance and administration. Sandy Swartzentruber, who had served since 1991 as director of publications, continued in that significant position. As board member Jay Kesler of Taylor University noted in an interview, the net effect of consolidation was to make the Coalition less staff-centered; power shifted noticeably to the president and the board.[6]

In October 1994 Andringa held a retreat for the Coalition's directors for the purposes of reorganizing the board and strengthening it as a policymaking group. The board adopted a new Standing Policies Manual that included sections on goals, board structure, relationships with the president, and financial and program guidelines. The manual provided a system of board committees and advisory councils (later commissions) that was keyed to the Coalition's organizational structure. One of the new entities, the Racial Harmony Council, represented one of the ways that the Coalition sought to maintain some of the diversity initiatives from the Augsburger presidency.[7]

In the interests of financial stability and image, Andringa and the board took some additional actions at the retreat. First, Andringa proposed and the board approved a fifty percent increase in dues paid by member institutions. Second, the group agreed to present a new corporate name—the Coalition for Christian Colleges & Universities—for consideration at the next annual meeting early in 1995. This change, which became official on March 1, 1995, recognized the fact that at least a score of the membership owned the "university" title. Furthermore, the new name was designed to set the association more clearly apart from both the Christian Coalition and the Christian College Consortium, albeit for different reasons. Finally, the addition of "universities" in the name prepared the way for international affiliate members, many of whom operated in parts of the world where the term "college" suggested a secondary school.[8]

The word "for" in the revised nomenclature in part reflected another proposal from the 1994 retreat. Andringa picked up on an earlier suggestion by Myron Augsburger that the Coalition create a special category for institutions that were striving to meet full membership requirements. For his part, Andringa envisioned such an associate status in much broader terms. The board ratified the idea and in 1995 the Coalition first accepted "non-member affiliate" institutions that were committed to distinctly Christian higher education. More than forty affiliates eventually came under the CCCU umbrella, including historically black colleges like Bethune-Cookman, theological seminaries such as Southwestern Baptist, international institutions like Tokyo Christian University, and one Roman Catholic school, the Franciscan University of Steubenville, Ohio. Affiliates pay reduced dues, attend the annual meetings, and have some opportunities to participate in CCCU programs.[9] Overall, their involvement has enhanced the cultural diversity and global outlook of the association.

At the same time, steady growth in regular membership once again highlighted the denominational pluralism of the CCCU. By early 2000, several schools joined for the first time from the following ecclesiastical traditions: Churches of Christ (Abilene Christian, Lipscomb, and Oklahoma Christian), Christian Church/Churches of Christ (Kentucky Christian), Southern Baptist (East Texas Baptist, Southwest Baptist, and Williams Baptist), Presbyterian (College of the Ozarks), and independent (William Tyndale). In the process of admitting new members, the board continued to review membership criteria, particularly in regard to offerings in the arts and sciences. In addition, the directors developed a succinct expression of the CCCU's mission statement: "Advance the cause of Christ-centered higher education and help our institutions effectively integrate biblical faith, scholarship and service."[10] Clearly the statement underlined many of the CCCU's historic purposes and thus helped to maintain continuity with the Dellenback and Augsburger eras.

In light of the Coalition's sustained growth, another Andringa idea proved to be felicitous. As part of the restructuring of the staff and board, the president began to organize volunteers to provide leadership and support for programs and services throughout the organization. Currently more than ninety volunteers, many from CCCU campuses, serve on committees, advisory commissions, or peer group commissions. That total number also includes individuals who have been designated for special service as advisors or fellows. Examples from these latter categories include Senior Advisor Richard Stephens, former president of Greenville College, Senior Fellow Harold Heie of

Gordon College, and Distinguished Senior Fellow Charles Colson of Prison Fellowship. The CCCU communicates with its volunteers through the *Volunteer Leader News*.[11]

In the eyes of many Christian college presidents, Andringa's greatest asset was that he knew his way around Washington.[12] For his part, the CCCU president summarized his perspective on government relations in a recent list of challenges that he drew up for leaders at member institutions:

> Almost every private college has become dependent on government student aid money. We must be involved, in non-partisan ways, in communicating needs common to all campuses as well as our specific, faith-related needs and concerns such as hiring and admissions policies. We can also contribute to civil society by articulating to the public the Christian worldview principles that we believe should guide difficult social issues. Our students need to be equipped to engage a pluralistic society, not become isolated from it.[13]

More like Dellenback than Augsburger in terms of political connections, Andringa invested time meeting with Secretary of Education Richard Riley and members of Congress, as well as with key congressional staff people. He also became very active in the National Association of Independent Colleges and Universities, serving on that agency's Commission for Financing Higher Education and Task Force on Lobbying. His recognition that Congress wanted the various higher education groups to develop common positions guided his efforts to align the CCCU with other associations whenever possible. Thus he sought to fulfill one of the Coalition's original mandates largely by being a supportive citizen of the national higher education community. His philosophy and networking approach paid off when the Coalition was invited to join the prestigious Washington Higher Education Secretariat in 1998.[14] This move further enhanced the CCCU's strategic presence in the nation's capital.

While Andringa's distinctive gifts and style meant new emphases, priorities, and structures, the Coalition was not so radically overhauled that it lost sight of its past. Like his predecessor, Andringa juggled traditional programs like the ASP, faculty development workshops, and publications with newer initiatives. Although he was not directly involved in the planning or execution of all the new ventures, his concern for quality and relevance certainly formed an overarching framework for what was developed.

New Student Programs

Under the leadership of Rich Gathro and Marge Bernbaum, who became full-time student programs manager in 1995, off-campus programs for students from Coalition colleges continued to increase. Although the organization has helped to sponsor the Carl F. H. Henry Scholarship in journalism since 1991, no curricular venture existed in that field until the summer of 1995, when the Coalition offered its first Summer Institute of Journalism in Washington. Funded by a grant from Fieldstead & Company, the "Capstone in the Capital" workshop incorporated seminars with media professionals and hands-on writing projects. Sue Crider of Houghton College and Terry Mattingly, then of Milligan College, designed a month-long pilot program to supplement journalism education at member institutions and to enhance the students' career preparation. Following the success of the first institute, the Student Academic Programs Council reviewed it favorably and the Coalition board approved it as a permanent program in early 1996. A second grant from the Scripps Howard Foundation allowed journalism professors to participate in a week of the SIJ during the summer of 1996. Terry Mattingly's role as a CCCU senior fellow has augmented the impact of this valuable endeavor, which embodies the association's long-term vision for cultural penetration and the integration of faith with learning.[15]

In July 1997 the Coalition's board of directors authorized two additional overseas programs for students. First, the Oxford Honours Programme expanded an earlier relationship with the Center for Medieval & Renaissance Studies (CMRS), an affiliate of Keble College at the University of Oxford. While the summer program continues, this more recent initiative offers participants a longer stay in England and combines two self-designed tutorials, an interactive seminar, and an integrative survey course. Intended for honors students, the Oxford semester requires a minimum 3.5 grade point average. The program opened in the fall of 1998 under the direction of John Frazier Jackson, a doctoral student at Oxford. It is currently headed by Stanley Rosenberg, a patristics scholar who also serves as vice principal of the CMRS.[16]

The China Studies Program (CSP) represented the second new international endeavor. The CSP started early in 1999 under the leadership of Chan Kim-Kwong, who was previously an honorary research fellow at the Chinese University of Hong Kong. Based at Shanghai's Fudan University, Xiamen University, and Xian Foreign Languages University, the program follows a curricular model similar to that of the LASP, the MESP, and the RSP. Students take seminars on China's culture, economics, history, geography, and politics; they also study standard Chinese, travel throughout the country, and engage in service projects. In the fall of 1999 Jay Lundelius, who earned a Ph.D. in second language acquisition at the University of Illinois, assumed responsibilities as CSP director. Dr. Chan became a CCCU senior fellow, and he continues to assist the program as a resource person and lecturer.[17]

By the year 2000 the CCCU was running two student programs in the United States (Washington and Los Angeles) and five in other parts of the world (China, Costa Rica, Egypt, England, and Russia), along with the summer sessions in Washington and Oxford. By the end of 2000, over four thousand students will have participated in these nine programs since the ASP started in 1976. Indeed, these offerings now constitute 58 percent of the budget, an indication of how prominent a place they have in the overall scheme of things. The CCCU also recognizes the following independent student programs: the AuSable Institute of Environmental Studies in Michigan, the Christian Center for Urban Studies in Chicago, the Focus on the Family Institute in Colorado, the Global Stewardship Study Program in Belize, the International Business Institute at King College, the Jerusalem University College in Israel, the Netherlandic Study Program in Contemporary Europe at Dordt College, the Romanian Studies Program at Eastern Nazarene College, EduVenture in Indonesia, and the San Francisco Urban Program of Westmont College.[18] Students from CCCU member institutions clearly enjoy a rich variety of options for off-campus study, which will be further enhanced when the Council launches a Contemporary Music Program in fall 2001.[19]

Professional Development

Bob Andringa and Karen Longman devoted considerable attention to strengthening the Coalition's professional development initiatives. Given his background as a consultant to nonprofit executives, it is not surprising that Andringa inaugurated a series of Presidents' Dialogues early in his presidency. In the summer of 1995 he and his wife Sue hosted presidents and spouses from Coalition schools at both Huntington College in Indiana and a resort in Frisco, Colorado; similar sessions followed the next two summers. While not aimed explicitly at professional development, the Dialogues provided college presidents with an informal setting in which to share concerns and build fellowship with peers.[20]

A more ambitious project emerged in 1995 when Barry and Sharon Hawes, CCCU friends from Vancouver, British Columbia, agreed to fund a peer-oriented training program that became known as the Executive Leadership Development Project (ELDP). Under the leadership of Don Page, vice president for academic affairs at Trinity Western University, the Executive Leadership Development Institute (ELDI) started with a Presidents' Institute at Frisco, Colorado, in July 1996. Coordinated by Rich Stephens, a CCCU senior advisor, the five-day gathering features seminars on the key roles of a college president. Stephens also matched newer presidents with more seasoned ones to initiate a two-year mentoring process. Eventually the ELDI concept expanded to include chief academic officers and "emerging leaders"; in the latter category, particular emphasis was placed on women and people of color. In fact, grants from the Kellogg and Mellon foundations in 1999 totaling $240,000 strengthened leadership development efforts involving women and minorities.[21] Along with previously established peer-group meetings that occur annually, the ELDI allows the CCCU to offer college executives and administrators a significant array of opportunities for personal and professional growth.

Faculty development likewise continued to be a vital part of CCCU programming. Steady funding from the Murdock Trust helped to sustain new faculty workshops, regional gatherings, and special meetings like the 1996 communication faculty conference at Calvin College, which was held in anticipation of the eighth installment in the Supplemental Textbook Series.[22] Then late in 1997 the John Templeton Foundation granted $800,000 for the Templeton Seminars on Science and Christianity, which began at the University of Oxford in 1999. Thirty professors in the sciences and religious studies, many from CCCU campuses, were chosen to spend a month participating in seminars and working on scholarly projects in Oxford for three successive summers. The steering committee explained that the main purpose of the program was "to introduce a greater scholarly rigour and authority into the study of the major issues in the relationship between science and religion."[23] This ongoing project holds tremendous potential for advancing the integration of faith and the various scientific disciplines.

An anonymous $1 million gift for a faculty development endowment in 1998 boosted the funding of a comprehensive program that the Faith/Learning/Living Commission designed. The Commission concluded that the CCCU needed a more multifaceted approach to faculty development; it sought to combine breadth and depth by giving attention to both teaching and scholarship. In particular, the Commission proposed regional workshops for new faculty, national faculty workshops in specific disciplines, advanced institutes on contemporary issues, and initiative grants to connect professors with common scholarly interests. While the institute idea is not yet funded and the disciplinary workshops have been delayed until 2001, the first initiative grants have been awarded and the regional workshops are on schedule.[24]

Finally, the CCCU launched a new campus-based faculty development program in May of 2000 with a five-day conference at Cornerstone University in Grand Rapids, Michigan. Planning and coordination of this three-year collaborative project fell largely to Dr. Ron Mahurin, who was named vice president for professional development and research in the fall of 1999 when Karen Longman left to become chief academic officer at Greenville College. He works closely with the program director, Gordon Van Harn, retired provost at Calvin College. Their stated goal is to "increase the quality, morale, and effectiveness of thousands of faculty by equipping their designated campus leaders to help plan and implement comprehensive, campus-specific faculty development strategies and activities." Almost seventy CCCU institutions have signed on, thereby agreeing to pay an annual fee that will help to fund the initiative. The CCCU expects each participating school to network with others in the program and share "best practices" that have been discovered through survey research and other assessment tools.[25] Although this endeavor is still in its infancy, it represents a fundamental shift in the way that the CCCU promotes faculty development.

Special Projects

Four special initiatives unfolded during the Andringa presidency, most of which received external funding. First, a $200,000 grant from

Pew Charitable Trusts enabled the Coalition to begin the two-year Global Stewardship Project early in 1995. This program, which involved twelve member campuses, called for interdisciplinary faculty research and curricular projects on environmental issues. Participating professors shared their findings and other information at three conferences. The project produced a statement—"Global Stewardship: The Christian Mandate"—which the board of directors endorsed in 1997.[26]

A second special initiative developed out of a growing interest in educational assessment among member institutions. Calvin College's Center for Christian Scholarship sponsored a conference on the assessment theme in the spring of 1993, which produced an important collection of essays, including some by authors from Coalition schools.[27] This conference also sparked a joint publishing venture by the Coalition and Messiah College that was inaugurated in 1994 with the first issue of *Research on Christian Higher Education*.[28] Edited by Messiah administrator Ron Burwell, this annual publication provides timely data from research projects, including reports on assessment activities at various CCCU campuses.

In the meantime, Karen Longman guided a Coalition Assessment Task Force to sponsor another conference at Calvin in 1994: "Comprehensive Assessment Plans for Christian Colleges." Moreover, Longman and Bayard Baylis, then associate dean at Messiah College, drew up a grant proposal to the Fund for the Improvement of Postsecondary Education (FIPSE) for a major project: "Taking Values Seriously: Assessing the Mission of Church-Related Higher Education." FIPSE, which operates under the U.S. Department of Education, awarded the Coalition $222,000 for a three-year collaborative study. The grant was announced at the 1994 Calvin conference.[29]

Extended by additional FIPSE grants of $258,000 in 1997 and $28,000 in 2000, the ongoing assessment effort combines quantitative and qualitative research on students, alumni, and faculty from fifty-three CCCU schools. For example, freshmen who entered college in 1994 participated in nationally normed surveys and videotaped interviews, which were repeated when they became seniors in 1998; follow-up alumni surveys were taken two years after graduation. Through this process, key researchers like Ron Burwell, John Van Wicklin of Houghton College, and Randall Bergen of Geneva College have focused especially on identifying any changes in students' attitudes, behaviors, and beliefs over a period of time. National and regional assessment conferences served to disseminate and interpret the research data.[30]

The assessment project has aimed primarily at helping CCCU institutions evaluate how effectively they fulfill their stated missions. Preliminary results, based on survey and interview data from over forty thousand constituents, indicate the following general trends at member schools: (1) most freshmen arrive on CCCU campuses with a "foreclosed" or borrowed faith; (2) students retain a strong faith through the college years; (3) students perform well academically; (4) students are more conservative than CCCU faculty; (5) satisfaction levels of faculty are high; (6) faculty are highly engaged in their professional lives; (7) older faculty are more productive and satisfied than younger faculty; and (8) the value that faculty place on minority education is not matched by institutional success in recruiting and supporting minority students.[31] In light of the CCCU's promotion of its overseas student programs, it is also revealing that students with cross-cultural exposure demonstrate much more "identity achievement" and a less "foreclosed" faith than those who lack such experiences.[32] As this longitudinal initiative proceeds and conclusions become more definitive, CCCU institutions should be in a much better position to assess how well they are performing and to what extent Christian higher education makes a difference.

The Collaborative Assessment Project also contributed to the birth of a related effort, the Quality/Retention Project. Brainstorming during an assessment conference at Cedarville College in 1996 suggested the need for more focus on retention as a key measure of institutional effectiveness. Consequently Karen Longman and Laurie Schreiner, a professor of psychology at Eastern College, developed a proposal for a new initiative, which the Coalition board approved early in 1997.[33]

Schreiner, who was appointed as project director, supervised a three-year project that began when the Noel-Levitz Student Satisfaction Survey was administered to almost twenty thousand students at seventy CCCU campuses in the fall of 1997. Data showed that CCCU students were more satisfied and content with their educational experiences than their counterparts at private secular schools, although the results did not fully explain dropout rates.[34]

As the project gathered momentum, it was enhanced through workshops, conferences, a newsletter, and a website; eventually eighty-five CCCU institutions became involved. Special emphases included improving academic advising during the second year and affirming students' strengths in the third. The latter focus prompted the use of the Gallup Organization's Strengths Finder on several campuses, as well as CCCU participation in the 2000 First-Year Experience Conference at the University of South Carolina. Later in 2000 the CCCU merged the assessment and retention efforts into a Combined Assessment Project.[35]

The Collaborative Assessment Project also inspired one other special initiative when it attracted the attention of James Fowler, a noted religious educator from Emory University who has developed a theory on the stages of faith development. Since the federal grants from FIPSE placed some constraints on researching spiritual growth, the CCCU consulted with Fowler in designing "Faithful Change: Assessing the Mission of Church-Related Higher Education." Fowler led a training program in 1998, and the new project was officially inaugurated in 1999 under the direction of Arthur Nonneman, a psychology professor at Asbury College, and Gay Holcomb, an associate in institutional research at Asbury. "Faithful Change" utilizes student interviews and surveys on eight CCCU campuses to assess how students shape their spiritual values and mature as Christians in a liberal arts setting. In June 2000 the Templeton Foundation announced a grant of $197,000 to help fund this innovative project.[36]

Programs dealing with global stewardship, institutional assessment, retention, and faith development illustrate the wide range of activities and services that the CCCU directs or sponsors. At the same time, these four endeavors, perhaps more than others, rely on cooperation and support from member schools. The success of these efforts points once again to the "movement" nature of the CCCU, one that draws strength from the "grass roots."

Technology

The Andringa era witnessed two major technology initiatives that further broadened the CCCU's agenda. First, the Coalition was accepted in 1995 as a member organization of the Gospel Communications Network, a step that established www.cccu.org as a new website. The site, which has been updated regularly, includes information about the CCCU and member schools, a calendar of events, job listings, networks of peer groups, and other useful resources for research. Late in

1998, the CCCU launched www.christiancollege.org, later changed to www.christiancollegesearch.com, as a tool for prospective students and their parents to access profiles of Christ-centered colleges and universities that fit specific criteria.[37]

In addition to its website development, the CCCU boldly plunged into computer-enhanced learning in 1998. A year earlier, Andringa floated a proposal to the board that the Coalition establish a separate distance-learning organization in partnership with a Christian-owned satellite firm in Florida. In response to the initial hesitation of some on the board, chairman James Bultman of Northwestern College in Iowa appointed a task force headed by Judson Carlberg, president of Gordon College. This group studied the idea and recommended that the board of directors approve the creation of a subsidiary nonprofit organization to foster collaborative educational efforts using computer technology. Early in 1998 the board accepted the task force's recommendation. Throughout the deliberations, Andringa sought to reassure some skeptical board members and institutional presidents, arguing that distance learning had the potential for "reaching tens of thousands of new adult learners who want something in cyberspace learning with a Christian worldview, and greatly increasing the visibility of our traditional programs."[38] By the end of 1998 the new subsidiary, the Christian University GlobalNet (CUGN), set up operations in Denver under the leadership of executive director Evan Morgan and chief academic officer Julie Jantzi, formerly of Western Baptist College (Oregon). Meanwhile, an anonymous $1.65 million grant greatly aided the development of this new initiative.[39]

CUGN, which itself does not grant credit or degrees, now maintains a common catalog of over 350 academic courses that are provided by over seventy participating CCCU schools. It also offers personal enrichment and certificate courses, conducts conferences, publishes a monthly newsletter, advertises a free filtered Internet service, seeks to facilitate faculty development in the production and use of distance learning, and makes available a digital archive of resources.[40] While this pioneering endeavor appears to hold enormous potential, some leaders on CCCU campuses have questioned whether it distracts from the CCCU mission or conflicts with institutional advertising that focuses on the personalized approach of residence-based learning.[41] From his perspective, however, Andringa confidently expects that

CUGN may turn out to be the most significant initiative to emerge during his presidency.[42]

Promotional Efforts

While the Coalition had been engaged in promotional activities from the very beginning, Bob Andringa assumed the presidency with some concerns about both the association's image and its overall fundraising strategies. Furthermore, the Coalition suffered a $350,000 setback with the collapse of the Foundation for New Era Philanthropy in 1995. Although a good portion of this loss was eventually recovered, the board authorized the sale of rental properties at 321–323 Eighth Street and the DeArmond House near the Capitol partly to ease the short-term financial pressures.[43]

As the Coalition began recovery from the New Era damage, public relations received fresh attention in 1995, as evidenced by the new website. In addition, Sue Crider of Houghton College spent her sabbatical helping the Coalition with promotional projects, and Jenifer Voskuil, a graduate of Taylor University, became the organization's first director of communications. Their work with media relations and publications helped lay the foundation for future initiatives.[44]

In July 1996, the board of directors authorized preliminary planning for a new campaign with a two-pronged purpose: "visibility of and funding for the improvement of Christ-centered higher education."[45] As the new drive officially kicked off in 1997, Andringa reiterated the need for the CCCU and its member campuses to "advance the cause" or "make the case"—terminology that continues to be used in this ongoing effort. When Voskuil left the Coalition to get married, Julie Peterson became the new director of communications with responsibility for some of the marketing aspects of the campaign. Charlotte Kroeker, a development officer for the Boyer Center at Messiah College and widow of Ken Shipps, was named part-time director of the United Christian College Fund (UCCF), which was established to solicit grants from foundations, corporations, and individuals. The Murdock Trust gave $200,000 to help launch the UCCF. Overall, the CCCU expected to strengthen itself and member schools through the campaign. In 2000 the board renamed this project the United Christian College Foundation with Gloria Gaither serving as chair and Lee

Noel as a trustee. The UCCF will likely become a separate nonprofit entity under the CCCU umbrella.[46]

Three important developments in 1998 contributed to the success of the CCCU's promotional and fundraising drive. First, the organization held its first National Forum on Christian Higher Education in Indianapolis in April, with over seven hundred participants. A much expanded version of the annual meeting, the forum was described by *The News* as "the largest gathering of Christian college faculty and administrators" in the Coalition's history. Plenary sessions and workshops served to highlight the CCCU's broad range of activities and interests; the meeting also demonstrated what Gordon Van Harn called the "maturity" of the association. A second forum has been scheduled for Orlando in 2001, when the CCCU will celebrate its silver anniversary.[47]

Second, at the April forum the Coalition announced a new cooperative venture with the Mustard Seed Foundation that would grant member institutions scholarship money for Hispanic, Native American, and African-American students. Priority would be given to schools that had participated in the earlier Racial and Ethnic Diversity Initiative. CCCU representatives later met with presidents of historically black colleges at the Carter Center in Atlanta.[48]

Finally, in mid-1998 the Coalition received the first installment of a $1.5 million anonymous grant to renovate and expand the repurchased facilities adjacent to The Dellenback Center. The gift called for a matching component, which was to be used for faculty development and promotional endeavors. The construction project was completed in early 2000, giving the CCCU more office space, a fitness center for ASP students, two apartments, and a video conferencing center that will allow for the production and transmission of programs from Washington.[49]

In 1999 the CCCU took further strides to enhance its image. The presidents' conference unanimously adopted the Council for Christian Colleges & Universities as the organization's new name, effective April 15. The second name change in four years was motivated once again by concerns that the CCCU was being confused "with more politically active organizations." Andringa specifically noted that "this confusion made it difficult for us to be understood by the media, foundations and the broader higher education community."[50] Follow-up initiatives in 1999 included the unveiling of a new logo and the designation of October as Christian Higher Education Month.[51] Clearly the CCCU had become more aggressive and intentional in its attempts to heighten public awareness of its mission. In this regard, it received a boost when secular media outlets reported that, between 1990 and 1996, enrollments at CCCU schools grew by 24 percent in comparison to a 5 percent growth rate at private colleges and 4 percent at public institutions.[52]

Some of the most recent CCCU activities hold direct, or at least indirect, relevance for "advancing the cause." Under the leadership of Julie Peterson, the Council began a $400,000 marketing research study of member institutions with Maguire, Inc. of Boston.[53] As a way of generating revenue and providing reduced rates for services to member schools, the Council has entered into business partnerships with entities like Sallie Mae, the National Higher Education Purchasing Consortium, Spectrum Marketing, AdTech International, and EdInsure. Further, Andringa enlisted Distinguished Senior Fellow Jay Kesler as a co-host for two-minute radio spots on Christian stations that would inform listeners about Christian higher education; the website for this program, which started in October of 2000, is www.ChristianCollegeTalk.com.

In some of his most recent efforts, the CCCU president is also working with Distinguished Senior Fellow Charles Colson on a collaborative project to promote Christian worldview thinking. Similarly, the CCCU and Baker Books are planning to advance the integration of faith and learning through RenewedMinds, a line of scholarly works and student textbooks.

At its summer 2000 retreat the CCCU board charged Andringa to "advance the cause" by (1) launching the United Christian College Foundation; (2) orienting the CCCU toward a more global perspective, including exchanges between member schools in the United States and international affiliates; and (3) developing new ways to make racial harmony a more urgent priority in Christian higher education.[54]

During the Andringa presidency, the CCCU has developed into a complex organization with over ninety distinct activities and projects supported by a budget that reached $7.7 million for fiscal 2000–2001; regular membership hit the century mark by August of 2000.[55] While maintaining traditional emphases on government relations, faculty development, and student programs, the Council has not hesitated to enlarge its base and expand its scope. Karen Longman refers to Andringa as the "consummate networker" and "maximizer," terms that aptly describe how he has managed the association since 1994.[56]

Although controversy accompanied some initiatives such as distance learning, overall the CCCU made definite progress in the fulfillment of its objectives.

A Final Word

For a quarter century the Coalition/CCCU has served the cause of distinctly Christian higher education in a host of ways. Through the leadership of CCCU presidents, staff, and board members, along with the support and participation of presidents, administrators, faculty, and students from member institutions, the organization has established a strategic presence and carved a unique niche in the wider educational community. As a result, Christ-centered postsecondary education is no longer marginalized; instead, it has emerged as a credible, visible, and viable enterprise. Faith-affirming colleges and universities have gained significant exposure, respect, and confidence as they seek to be "shining lights" in a challenging cultural setting.

The mutually supportive relationship that exists between the CCCU and its member schools points to the association's important catalytic role. While the CCCU provides substantial leadership and direction, it also inspires and empowers many of its constituents to assume major responsibilities in carrying out various projects and initiatives. The networks that the CCCU has facilitated and helped to sustain illuminate the vitality of what is truly, in the words of John Bernbaum, a "movement."[57]

Beyond its strategic and catalytic roles, the CCCU also functions as an exemplary model in three meaningful ways. First, the organization's faculty development workshops, scholarly publications, and student programs encourage intellectual and cultural engagement. While there is still much to be done to overcome the "scandal"[58] of the evangelical mind, the CCCU's long-term commitment to the integration of faith and learning has contributed to advances in evangelical scholarship. At the same time, it is not clear that all presidents and faculty at member institutions understand or appreciate the value of integrative approaches. Even though the recent enthusiasm about technology is understandable, the Council will need to work hard to balance innovative techniques with more traditional emphases in the area of faculty development. Further, the CCCU may need to refresh its schools

95

on the urgency of a cultural, intellectual, and theological vision to sustain genuinely Christian higher education in a postmodern society.[59]

As it fosters cultural and intellectual pursuits, the CCCU also demonstrates an ecumenical spirit that unites a diverse group of schools in the pursuit of a common cause. While evangelicalism seems increasingly fragmented, collaboration in the CCCU has created some enduring bonds that might suggest some direction for the wider evangelical community as what George Brushaber calls the "Graham consensus" weakens.[60] By bringing its disparate constituents together, the CCCU has assisted them in achieving far more than would have been the case had they labored separately.

Finally, the association's cross-cultural and international initiatives remind American evangelicals that Christianity is a global faith that transcends all national, racial, and ethnic boundaries. This dimension of the CCCU agenda has been reinforced in recent years with the admission of many affiliates from other countries. In cultivating a worldwide perspective and showing that educational agencies can play a part in articulating and applying the gospel of Jesus Christ, the CCCU has rendered valuable service to the kingdom.

When Carl Henry and the founders of the Christian College Consortium dreamed of a major Christian university in the 1960s and early 1970s, it is unlikely that they envisioned a confederation of one hundred decentralized, autonomous campuses joined together for the advancement of Christian higher learning. John Dellenback, however, suggests that the CCCU has developed into a "great university"; or, more precisely, it functions as an appropriate, workable alternative to the unfulfilled hope of a previous era.[61] The former president's perceptive remarks represent a fitting tribute to the organization as it celebrates twenty-five years of notable achievements and looks ahead to an enhanced entrepreneurial role in the dynamic world of Christian higher education.

Notes

Preface

1. See Philip Gleason, *Contending with Modernity: Catholic Higher Education in the Twentieth Century* (New York: Oxford, 1995); George M. Marsden, *The Soul of the American University: From Protestant Establishment to Established Nonbelief* (New York: Oxford, 1994); and Douglas Sloan, *Faith and Knowledge: Mainline Protestantism and American Higher Education* (Louisville: Westminster/John Knox, 1994).

2. James Tunstead Burtchaell, *The Dying of the Light: The Disengagement of Colleges and Universities from Their Christian Churches* (Grand Rapids: Eerdmans, 1998), xii. See also Burtchaell, "The Decline and Fall of the Christian College," *First Things*, no. 12 (April 1991): 16–29; and no. 13 (May 1991): 30–38.

3. Burtchaell, *The Dying of the Light*, 743–817.

4. The CCCU has had three names in its twenty-five year history. For the sake of historical accuracy, this book uses the "Christian College Coalition" for the period 1976–95, the "Coalition for Christian Colleges & Universities" (CCCU) for the period 1995–99, and the "Council for Christian Colleges & Universities" (also CCCU) for the period 1999–2001 and for general statements that span the entire history of the organization.

Chapter 1

1. D. A. Carson, "Can There Be a Christian University?" *Southern Baptist Journal of Theology* 1 (Fall 1997): 26–33. Carson advances two other theses not cited here because they are more applicable to universities in general, whereas the ones listed bear relevance for distinctly Christian colleges and universities.

2. Arthur F. Holmes, "Augustine of Hippo on Liberal Arts Education" (lecture presented as Scholar-in-Residence at Union University, Jackson, Tenn., 3 March 2000).

3. Carson, "Can There Be a Christian University?" 20.

4. John Van Engen, "Christianity and the University: The Medieval and Reformation Legacies," in *Making Higher Education Christian: The History and Mission of Evangelical Colleges in America*, eds. Joel A. Carpenter and Kenneth W. Shipps (Grand Rapids: Christian University Press/Eerdmans, 1987), 19–37.

5. George M. Marsden, *The Soul of the American University: From Protestant Establishment to Established Nonbelief* (New York: Oxford, 1994), 38–42.

6. Leland Ryken, "Reformation and Puritan Ideals of Education," in *Making Higher Education Christian*, 48.

7. "New England's First Fruits [1643]," in *The Puritans: A Sourcebook of Their Writings*, rev. ed., eds. Perry Miller and Thomas H. Johnson (New York: Harper Torchbooks, 1963), 2:702.

8. On the founding of Yale as a counter to Harvard, see Marsden, *The Soul of the American University*, 52–53.

9. William C. Ringenberg, *The Christian College: A History of Protestant Higher Education in America* (Grand Rapids: Christian University Press/Eerdmans, 1984), 39–41.

10. Marsden, *The Soul of the American University*, 42–44.

11. Ringenberg, *The Christian College*, 41–42.

12. Ibid., 37.

13. On the significance of the Second Great Awakening for higher education, see Ringenberg, *The Christian College*, 56–60.

14. Mark A. Noll, "The Revolution, the Enlightenment, and Christian Higher Education in the Early Republic," in *Making Higher Education Christian*, 59–64. "Didactic" is one of four categories for the Enlightenment used in Henry F. May, *The Enlightenment in America* (New York: Oxford, 1976).

15. Noll, "The Revolution," 70–71.

16. Ibid., 64.

17. See Noll's follow-up essay, "The University Arrives in America, 1870–1930: Christian Traditionalism during the Academic Revolution," in *Making Higher Education Christian*, 98–109.

18. Many of these changes are discussed in Ringenberg, *The Christian College*, 115–21.

19. Mark A. Noll, "Christian Colleges, Christian Worldviews, and an Invitation to Research," in Ringenberg, *The Christian College*, 29. The most complete account of secularization is found in Marsden, *The Soul of the American University*, especially chapters 5–14.

20. Noll, "Christian Colleges," 24–27.

21. On the intellectual crises of Christian higher education, see Marsden, *The Soul of the American University*, 93; and Mark A. Noll, *The Scandal of the Evangelical Mind* (Grand Rapids: Eerdmans, 1994), 100–107. On seminaries as places of theological reflection apart from colleges and universities, see Noll, "Christian Colleges," 20–24.

22. Marsden, *The Soul of the American University*, 5.

23. Carson, "Can There Be a Christian University?" 35.

24. Ringenberg, *The Christian College*, 85–91.

25. For a concise overview of the Bible college movement, see Virginia Lieson Brereton, "The Bible Schools and Conservative Evangelical Higher Education, 1880–1940," in *Making Higher Education Christian*, 110–36.

26. On Wheaton and fundamentalism, see Ringenberg, *The Christian College*, 173–74.

27. Noll, *The Scandal of the Evangelical Mind*, 109–45.

28. For discussions of identities of various schools, see Brereton, "The Bible Schools," 113; Joel A. Carpenter, *Revive Us Again: The Reawakening of American Fundamentalism* (New York: Oxford, 1997), 21; and Ringenberg, *The Christian College*, 100–102, 174–76.

29. Carpenter, *Revive Us Again*, 9.

30. Carl F. H. Henry, *Remaking the Modern Mind* (Grand Rapids: Eerdmans, 1946); and idem., *The Uneasy Conscience of Modern Fundamentalism* (Grand Rapids: Eerdmans, 1947).

31. Carpenter, *Revive Us Again*, especially chapters 8, 9, and 12.

32. Thomas A. Askew, "The Shaping of Evangelical Higher Education since World War II," in *Making Higher Education Christian*, 139–41. Yale philosopher Nicholas Wolterstorff speaks of Christian colleges going "underground" during "Stage I," or the period between about 1900 and 1945. See "The Mission of the Christian College at the End of the 20th Century," *Reformed Journal* 33 (June 1983): 14.

33. Askew, "Evangelical Higher Education," 140.

34. Ringenberg, *The Christian College*, 188.

35. Ibid., 188–89; and Askew, "Evangelical Higher Education," 137–38.

36. Askew, "Evangelical Higher Education," 141–46. Much of what follows is drawn from this material. The period that Askew describes is roughly equivalent to what Wolterstorff calls "Stage II." See Wolterstorff's "The Mission of the Christian College at the End of the 20th Century," 15–16.

37. Askew, "Evangelical Higher Education," 145–46.

38. Ibid., 141–44.

39. Ibid., 142.

40. Ibid., 143. On the early history of the Council, see Alfred T. Hill, *The Small College Meets the Challenge: The Story of CASC* (New York: McGraw-Hill, 1959).

Chapter 2

1. For both of these illustrations, see Harold William Berk, "The Christian College Consortium in Social Context" (Ph.D. diss., University of Toledo, 1974), 66.

2. Carl F. H. Henry, "Why Not a Federated Campus?" *Christianity Today*, 19 January 1962, 24.

3. Carl F. H. Henry, "The Power of the Truth," *Christianity Today*, 13 September 1963, 26.

4. Cf. Carl F. H. Henry, "Evangelical Colleges as Faith-Affirming Institutions," *Christianity Today*, 10 September 1965, 25–26; and Manning M. Pattillo Jr. and Donald M. Mackenzie, *Church-Sponsored Higher Education in the United States: Report of the Danforth Commission* (Washington, D.C.: American Council on Education, 1966), 192–93, 197 n. 1.

5. Robert S. Lutz, "'National University' Proposed at NAE," *Christianity Today*, 13 May 1966, 47–48.

6. On the associational idea of the Commission, see J. Richard Chase, draft outline of address to Christian College Coalition, February 1986, CCCU archives, Washington, D.C.; and Karen A. Longman, "Celebrating Twenty Years of Service, 1976–1996," unpublished manuscript, 1, CCCU archives, Washington, D.C.

7. Carl F. H. Henry, telephone interview by author, 28 January 2000. See also George M. Marsden, "Why No Evangelical University? The Loss and Recovery of Evangelical Advanced Scholarship," in *Making Higher Education Christian: The History and Mission of Evangelical Colleges in America*, eds. Joel A. Carpenter and Kenneth W. Shipps (Grand Rapids: Christian University Press/Eerdmans, 1987), 298.

8. Carl F. H. Henry, "The Need for a Christian University," *Christianity Today*, 17 February 1967, 7–8.

9. On the Indiana seminar, see Berk, "The Christian College Consortium," 74; James Carl Hendrix, "The Christian College Consortium: 1971–1991" (Ph.D. diss., Southern Illinois University at Carbondale, 1992), 45–46; and John W. Snyder, "Why Not a Christian College on a University Campus?" *Christianity Today*, 17 February 1967, 14–17. Additional

information came from Hudson T. Armerding, telephone interview by author, 17 February 2000; and David L. McKenna, telephone interview by author, 1 March 2000.

10. Henry, interview.

11. Carl F. H. Henry, *Confessions of a Theologian: An Autobiography* (Waco: Word, 1986), 341–44.

12. Thomas A. Askew, "The Shaping of Evangelical Higher Education since World War II," in *Making Higher Education Christian*, 146–48.

13. Ibid., 148.

14. See George Brushaber's editorial, *Christian Scholar's Review* 1 (Fall 1970): 3–4.

15. Armerding, interview; Hendrix, "Consortium: 1971–1991," 46.

16. On the initial planning for the Tempe conference, see Berk, "The Christian College Consortium," 75, 280–81; and Hendrix, "Consortium: 1971–1991," 46–47.

17. Berk, "The Christian College Consortium," 76–77.

18. Earl McGrath, quoted in David Kucharsky, "Evangelical Colleges Plan Consortium," *Christianity Today*, 9 April 1971, 45.

19. Berk, "The Christian College Consortium," 277; and Hendrix, "Consortium: 1971–1991," 34–35.

20. Carl F. H. Henry, "The Rationale of the Christian College," *Christianity Today*, 21 May 1971, 10.

21. Carl F. H. Henry, "Faith-Affirming Colleges," *Christianity Today*, 7 May 1971, 33.

22. Hendrix, "Consortium: 1971–1991," 47–48.

23. Ibid., 49; and Berk, "The Christian College Consortium," 281.

24. For early organizational information, see Hendrix, "Consortium: 1971–1991," 49–50.

25. Quoted in ibid., 67.

26. Two schools that participated in the Tempe conference were not among the charter members. Oklahoma Christian never joined the Consortium and Asbury delayed its entrance until 1976. See ibid., 120, 126.

27. Ibid., 108.

28. Timothy L. Smith, "The Evangelical Kaleidoscope and the Call to Christian Unity," *Christian Scholar's Review* 15 (1986): 125–40. On the Consortium's denominational variety, see Timothy L. Smith, "Introduction: Christian Colleges and American Culture," in *Making Higher Education Christian*, 1–2.

29. Hendrix, "Consortium: 1971–1991," 113.

30. On membership changes, see ibid., 126–27.

31. Quoted in ibid., 73.

32. On Neteland, see ibid., 50, 74–75, 92–94; and "What's New: Christian Higher Education," *Christianity Today*, 24 September 1971, 44–45.

33. Hendrix, "Consortium: 1971–1991," 72.

34. David L. McKenna, "Consortium Chairman Calls Schools to Task of Integration, Confrontation," *Universitas*, special issue (March 1972): 1.

35. Hendrix, "Consortium: 1971–1991," 95–96.

36. On the workshops, see ibid., 146–49; and "Faith/Learning/Living Seminar Planned for Summer," *Christian College News Service*, 22 April 1977, 1–2.

37. For some insights on Henry, I am indebted to Arthur F. Holmes, interview by author, 7 March 2000, Jackson, Tenn.

38. Michael S. Hamilton and James A. Mathisen, "Faith and Learning at Wheaton College," in *Models for Christian Higher Education: Strategies for Survival and Success in the*

Twenty-First Century, eds. Richard T. Hughes and William B. Adrian (Grand Rapids: Eerdmans, 1997), 279. Earlier Gaebelein wrote *The Pattern of God's Truth: The Integration of Faith and Learning* (New York: Oxford, 1954). Wheaton's interest in integration is evident in Hudson T. Armerding, ed., *Christianity and the World of Thought* (Chicago: Moody, 1968).

39. Arthur F. Holmes, *The Idea of a Christian College* (Grand Rapids: Eerdmans, 1975), 60. On Holmes and the Wheaton seminar, see Hamilton and Mathisen, "Faith and Learning at Wheaton College," 279–80.

40. Nicholas Wolterstorff, "The Mission of the Christian College at the End of the 20th Century," *Reformed Journal* 33 (June 1983): 15.

41. James D. Bratt and Ronald A. Wells, "Piety and Progress: A History of Calvin College," in *Models for Christian Higher Education*, 158–62; Ronald A. Wells, interview by author, 13 July 1999, Grand Rapids, Mich.; and Gordon R. Werkema, telephone interview by author, 15 February 2000.

42. Hendrix, "Consortium, 1971–1991," 97.

Chapter 3

1. On the Werkema appointment and change of title, see James Carl Hendrix, "The Christian College Consortium: 1971–1991" (Ph.D. diss., Southern Illinois University at Carbondale, 1992),75–76, 97.

2. Gordon R. Werkema, telephone interview by author, 15 February 2000.

3. Margery S. Bernbaum, interview by author, 1 February 2000, Washington, D.C.; Richard F. Gross, telephone interview by author, 23 February 2000; D. Ray Hostetter, telephone interview by author, 19 February 2000.

4. Hendrix, "Consortium: 1971–1991," 98; and "Christian University Press Names First Releases," *Christian College News Service*, 25 February 1977, 2–3.

5. Gordon R. Werkema, "Proposals for 1975–1980: Growing in Service to the Master, His People, and His World through the Ministry of Christian Higher Education," Christian College Consortium, 5–6 February 1975, 16. This and all succeeding citations of Consortium reports and minutes come from photocopies of originals in Consortium archives, Dunbarton, N.H.

6. Gordon R. Werkema, "Report of the President to the Board of Directors of the Christian College Consortium," 25 March 1975, 11.

7. Minutes of the Executive Committee of the Deans' Council, Christian College Consortium, 11 June 1975, 4, and 11 August 1975, 1; and Minutes of the Deans' Council, Christian College Consortium, 2 October 1975, 1. On the formation of the Deans' Council, see Hendrix, "Consortium: 1971–1991," 78–79.

8. Information on the Bernbaum appointment came from John A. Bernbaum, interview by author, 1 February 2000, Washington, D.C.; Werkema, interview; and Karen A. Longman, "Celebrating Twenty Years of Service, 1976–1996," unpublished manuscript, 2–3, CCCU archives, Washington, D.C.

9. Details on the early facilities came from Margery S. Bernbaum, interview. For the comment on community, see Gordon R. Werkema, "Semi-Annual Report to the Board of Directors of the Christian College Consortium," 3 March 1977, 12.

10. John A. Bernbaum, interview.

11. Gordon R. Werkema, "Report of the President, Christian College Consortium, to the Executive Board," 12 August 1975, 6.

12. Quoted in "Students View American Culture from Christian Perspective," *Christian College News Service*, 20 August 1976, 3.

13. Gordon R. Werkema, "Semi-Annual Report to the Board of Directors of the Christian College Consortium," 12 October 1977, 2. See also Werkema's press release, *Christian College Consortium News*, 7 February 1977, 1–2.

14. Margery S. Bernbaum, interview.

15. Minutes of the Executive Committee of the Board of Directors, Christian College Consortium, 28 June 1978, 3. On the Latin American proposal, see Werkema, "Semi-Annual Report to the Directors of the Christian College Consortium," 12 October 1977, 2–6; and "Latin American Studies, Language Center Established at Central America University," *Christian College News Service*, 4 November 1977, 2–3.

16. A brief overview of the Far East studies concept can be found in Werkema, "Semi-Annual Report to the Directors," 12 October 1977, 6.

17. W. Richard Stephens, interview by author, 31 January 2000, Washington, D.C.

18. From a copy of a letter that Chamberlain attached to correspondence with Robert Andringa, current president of the CCCU. Daniel R. Chamberlain, Houghton, N.Y., to Robert C. Andringa, Washington, D.C., 8 September 1999.

19. Hudson T. Armerding, telephone interview by author, 17 February 2000.

20. David L. McKenna, telephone interview by author, 1 March 2000.

21. William C. Ringenberg, *The Christian College: A History of Higher Education in America* (Grand Rapids: Christian University Press/Eerdmans, 1984), 211. For a helpful overview of church/state matters, see David K. Winter, "Rendering unto Caesar: The Dilemma of College-Government Relations," in *Making Higher Education Christian: The History and Mission of Evangelical Colleges in America*, eds. Joel A. Carpenter and Kenneth W. Shipps (Grand Rapids: Christian University Press/Eerdmans, 1987), 244–56.

22. Ringenberg, *The Christian College*, 213.

23. McKenna, interview. Ironically, McKenna was a finalist for Secretary of Education in 1980 when Ronald Reagan was putting together his cabinet.

24. George K. Brushaber, interview by author, 1 February 2000, Washington, D.C.

25. Minutes of the Executive Committee of the Christian College Consortium, 14 January 1975.

26. Gordon R. Werkema, "Proposals for 1975–1980," Christian College Consortium, 5–6 February 1975.

27. Minutes of the Board of Directors of the Christian College Consortium, 26 March 1975.

28. Gordon R. Werkema, "Report of the President to the Board of Directors of the Christian College Consortium," 10 October 1975, 5.

29. Ibid., 5–6.

30. On facilities, see Longman, "Celebrating Twenty Years of Service," 2.

31. "Description of the Christian College Coalition Proposed by the Christian College Consortium," January 1976, 1–2.

32. Gordon R. Werkema, "Report to the Annual Meeting of the Christian College Consortium," 2 March 1976.

33. "Christian College Coalition Information Sheet," Christian College Consortium, July 1976, 2.

34. Ibid., 1.

35. Kenneth L. Woodward, et al., "Born Again!" *Newsweek*, 25 October 1976, 69.

36. Werkema, interview.

37. None of the available documents specify exactly what colleges gathered at the Washington meeting. In fact, early records are fuzzy on the membership question. The identity of the earliest members has to be inferred from items in the *Christian College News Service* and from other, unpublished materials. A further complication is that some early Coalition members dropped out in the first few years, including Anderson (Church of God, Anderson, Ind.), Barrington (an independent school which later merged with Gordon), Grand Canyon (Southern Baptist), Grove City (Presbyterian), King (Presbyterian), Mid-America Nazarene (Church of the Nazarene), Mississippi (Southern Baptist), North Park (Evangelical Covenant), and Tennessee Temple (independent). Many of these eventually rejoined. Another early member, King's College in New York, is now operated by Campus Crusade and is not affiliated with the CCCU.

38. "Christian College Coalition Organizational Meeting, September 21–22, 1976," agenda, 1; and outline, 1. These and all succeeding citations of Coalition/CCCU reports and minutes are from photocopies of originals in CCCU archives, Washington, D.C.

39. "Christian College Coalition Formed," *Christian College News Service*, 1 October 1976, 2.

40. Gordon R. Werkema, "Semi-Annual Report to the Board of Directors of the Christian College Consortium," 8 October 1976, 5.

41. "Summary of the Organizational Meeting of the Christian College Coalition Board," 23 November 1976, 1–4.

42. Minutes of the Board of Directors of the Christian College Coalition, 11 February 1977, 1–4.

43. Gordon R. Werkema, "Semi-Annual Report to the Board of Directors of the Christian College Consortium," 3 March 1977, 3.

44. Stephens, interview.

45. "Search Committee Seeking Person for Top Post in Christian College Consortium," *Christian College News Service*, 23 September 1977, 6–7.

Chapter 4

1. Information on the selection of Dellenback came from "Search Committee Seeking Person for Top Post in Christian College Consortium," *Christian College News Service*, 23 September 1977, 6; D. Ray Hostetter, telephone interview by author, 19 February 2000; David C. LeShana, telephone interview by author, 1 March 2000; and David K. Winter, interview by author, 1 February 2000, Washington, D.C. For the tap dancing anecdote, see Karen A. Longman, "Celebrating Twenty Years of Service, 1976–1996," unpublished manuscript, 3, CCCU archives, Washington, D.C.

2. Biographical data came from John R. Dellenback, telephone interview by author, 29 January 2000.

3. Ibid. On the part-time nature of Dellenback's Coalition Salary, see his draft of a memorandum to the National Advisory Board, 30 June 1981, 2, CCCU archives, Washington, D.C.

4. John A. Bernbaum, interview by author, 1 February 2000, Washington, D.C.; Margery S. Bernbaum, interview by author, 1 February 2000, Washington, D.C.; and Karen A. Longman, interview by author, 25 March 2000, Greenville, Ill.

5. Richard Gathro, interview by author, 27 January 2000, Washington, D.C.

6. Ibid.

7. Richard Kriegbaum, "Christian Colleges: Some Will Not Survive," *Christianity Today*, 12 November 1982, 36.

8. Minutes of the Board of Directors, Christian College Coalition, 28 October 1980, 1.

9. See promotional letter, Christian College Coalition, February 1980, 3, CCCU archives, Washington, D.C.

10. "Christian College Coalition Files Amicus Curiae Brief on Behalf of Mississippi College in 'Discrimination' Case," *Christian College News Service*, 16 March 1979, 3–4. For a similar case involving staff hiring, see "Court Rules with Seattle Pacific in Employment Practices Dispute," *Christian College News*, April 1986, 1.

11. John R. Dellenback as quoted in "National Congress Brings Together Top Representatives of Church-Related Schools, Including Those of Coalition," *Christian College News*, 8 February 1980, 3.

12. On the Hatfield Amendment, see John R. Dellenback, "'Round One' Seeking Law Establishing Student Aid as That, Not Aid to College, Loses in Senate; But Efforts Continue," *Christian College News*, 11 July 1980, 2. Information on the Grove City case came from Dellenback, interview; and David K. Winter, "Rendering unto Caesar: The Dilemma of College-Government Relations," *Making Higher Education Christian: The History and Mission of Evangelical Colleges in America*, eds. Joel A. Carpenter and Kenneth W. Shipps (Grand Rapids: Christian University Press/Eerdmans, 1987), 245, 248, 255–56. In 1988, around the time Dellenback left the Coalition, Congress passed the Civil Rights Restoration Act to overturn the "program specific" part of the Supreme Court's 1984 ruling. See Charles MacKenzie, "Just Say No to Uncle Sam's Money," *Christianity Today*, 2 September 1988, 12.

13. "Newly-Formed Coalition Committee Considers Issues at Initial Meeting," *Christian College News*, July 1983, 2; W. Richard Stephens, interview by author, 31 January 2000, Washington, D.C.; and Minutes of the Board of Directors, Christian College Coalition, 23–24 January 1984, 3–4.

14. Dellenback, interview; H. David Brandt, interview by author, 31 January 2000, Washington, D.C.

15. Minutes of the Board of Directors, Christian College Coalition, 28 October 1980, 2; and Minutes of the Executive Committee, Christian College Consortium, 29 October 1980, 1.

16. Minutes of the Christian College Consortium Retreat, 10–13 March 1981, 1–2.

17. Minutes of the Executive Committee, Christian College Consortium, 25 March 1981, 1.

18. Ibid., 2.

19. Minutes of the Board of Directors, Christian College Coalition, 20 May 1981, 1–2.

20. Minutes of the Board of Directors, Christian College Consortium, 3 June 1981, 1.

21. Ibid., 2.

22. Daniel R. Chamberlain, telephone interview by author, 14 February 2000.

23. Brandt, interview.

24. George K. Brushaber, interview by author, 1 February 2000, Washington, D.C.

25. Minutes of the Executive Committee, Christian College Consortium, 14 October 1981, 1–2.

26. Information on the Consortium since 1981 came from James Carl Hendrix, "The Christian College Consortium: 1971–1991" (Ph.D. diss., Southern Illinois University at Carbondale, 1992), 103–6, 157–65; and Thomas H. Englund, interview by author, 19 November 1999, Concord, N.H.

27. On the official incorporation, see Minutes of the Board of Directors, Christian College Coalition, 2 February 1982, 1.

28. "Early Coalition Growth—Prospects," file folder in CCCU archives, Washington, D.C.

29. Dellenback, interview. He also used the "critical mass" phrase in this interview.

30. Minutes of the Board of Directors, Christian College Coalition, 28 October 1980, 1–2. For an example of Dellenback's use of "Christ-centered," see "'Christ-Centeredness' Distinguishes Christian Colleges from Other Schools," *Christian College News Service*, 21 April 1978, 5.

31. Longman, "Celebrating Twenty Years of Service," 3, 5.

32. Membership data was gathered from selected issues of the *Christian College News Service* and the *Christian College News* between 1978 and 1987.

33. For example, see Minutes of the Board of Directors, Christian College Coalition, 30 November 1981, 3–4; and 31 January–1 February 1988, 1–3.

34. Minutes of the Board of Directors, Christian College Coalition, 29–30 September 1986, 2–3; and 20–21 April 1987, 1. Some schools from the Churches of Christ eventually came in during the 1990s.

35. John A. Bernbaum, interview.

36. "January 1980 A.S.P. Interterm Approved; Open to 35 Students," *Christian College News Service*, 10 August 1979, 7; John A. Bernbaum, "Report on the Faculty Seminar on International Affairs," *Christian College News*, 3 October 1980, 1a–2a; and idem., "New Summer Internship Program Established in Washington," *Christian College News*, 28 November 1980, 1a.

37. Gathro, interview.

38. Jerry S. Herbert, telephone interview by author, 28 January 2000.

39. Quoted in "American Studies Program Celebrates Ten Years in the Nation's Capitol," *Christian College News*, June 1986, 1.

40. Steve Garber, "Developing Both Competence and Commitment in the Undergraduate," *Eternity*, September 1987, 25–26.

41. Minutes of the Board of Directors, Christian College Coalition, 28–29 January 1985, 5.

42. "Coalition to Launch Latin American Studies Program," *Christian College News*, October 1985, 1.

43. "Hoksbergen Selected Director of Latin American Studies Program," *Christian College News*, February 1986, 1–2.

44. "Latin American Studies Program Launched in Costa Rica," *Christian College News*, October 1986, 1–2.

45. "Staff Changes Announced: New Program Assistant Named," *Christian College News*, 5 September 1980, 5; Gathro, interview; and Longman, interview.

46. Karen A. Longman, "Integrating Faith, Learning, Living was Institute Goal at Trinity College," *Christian College News*, 11 September 1981, 2.

47. Minutes of the Board of Directors, Christian College Coalition, 30 November 1981, 5.

48. Longman, "Celebrating Twenty Years of Service," 3. For the grant announcement, see "Faculty at Christian College Coalition Institutions to Benefit from Grant," *Christian College News*, July 1982, 1.

49. "Month-Long Institute Concludes Endowment/Coalition Christianity and Humanities Project," *Christian College News*, August 1984, 1–2.

50. "Coalition Given $60,000 Grant by Murdock Trust of Vancouver," *Christian College News*, 24 February 1984, 2.

51. "Second Series of Workshops on Christianity/Liberal Arts Being Funded by Foundation," *Christian College News*, 1 October 1984, 1–2.

52. John R. Dellenback, "Publication of 'Christian College Guide' under Serious Consideration by Coalition," *Christian College News*, 4 April 1980, 2.

53. Minutes of the Board of Directors, Christian College Coalition, 30 November 1981, 1.

54. Karen A. Longman, ed., *A Guide to Christian Colleges* (Grand Rapids: Eerdmans, 1982). See also "Coalition's *Guide to Christian Colleges* Rolls off the Press at Wm. B. Eerdmans," *Christian College News*, 18 December 1981, 2.

55. "*A Guide to Christian Colleges*," *The Christian College Coalition: 1984 in Review*, 1.

56. *Consider a Christian College* (Princeton: Peterson's Guides, 1988); and "Peterson's To Produce Coalition Guide," *Christian College News*, November 1987, 1. On the Maclellan-funded national marketing initiative, see "College-Bound Students Surveyed about Christ-Centered Liberal Arts," *Christian College News*, December 1986, 1–2; and "Coalition Launches National Marketing Initiative," *Christian College News*, September 1987, 1.

57. *Choose a Christian College* (Princeton: Peterson's Guides, 1996); and *Peterson's Guide to Christian Colleges and Universities: Top Institutions Committed to Academic Quality and Character Development* (Princeton: Peterson's Guides, 1998).

58. "Messiah College Professor First Sabbatical Participant," *Christian College News*, 9 September 1983, 1; and Dean Curry, ed., *Evangelicals and the Bishops' Pastoral Letter* (Grand Rapids: Eerdmans, 1984). For books produced by Coalition staff, see John A. Bernbaum, ed., *Perspectives on Peacemaking: Biblical Options in the Nuclear Age* (Ventura, Calif.: Regal, 1984); and Jerry S. Herbert, ed., *America, Christian or Secular?: Readings in American Christian History and Civil Religion* (Portland, Oreg.: Multnomah, 1984).

59. John A. Bernbaum, ed., *Economic Justice and the State: A Debate between Ronald H. Nash and Eric H. Beversluis* (Grand Rapids: Baker, 1986); and John A. Bernbaum and Simon M. Steer, *Why Work? Careers and Employment in Biblical Perspective* (Grand Rapids: Baker, 1986).

60. "Coalition Releases First in Study Guide Series," *Christian College News*, September 1986, 2.

61. Augustus Cerillo Jr. and Murray W. Dempster, *Salt and Light: Evangelical Political Thought in Modern America* (Grand Rapids: Baker, 1989).

62. Minutes of the Board of Directors, Christian College Coalition, 19–20 September 1983, 5.

63. "Supplemental Textbooks From Christian Perspective under Consideration for Coalition Member Colleges," *Christian College News*, 30 March 1984, 5.

64. "Supplemental Textbook Project," *The Christian College Coalition: 1984 in Review*, 1; and Nicholas Wolterstorff, interview by author, 14 July 1999, Grand Rapids, Mich.

65. "Supplemental Text Project Off and Running," *The Christian College Coalition: 1985 in Review*, 1.

66. "Professors Explore Links between Psychology and Christian Faith," *Christian College News*, August 1986, 1. The time and energy that went into the Supplemental Series probably helps to explain why the Coalition board, three months after the psychology conference, rejected an overture from the Consortium to absorb the Christian University Press. See Minutes of the Board of Directors, Christian College Coalition, 29–30 September 1986, 6.

67. "Professors Look at Biology through the Eyes of Faith," *Christian College News*, July 1987, 1–2; and "Literature Conference Boasts Record Attendance," *The News*, December 1987, 1–2.

68. David G. Myers and Malcolm A. Jeeves, *Psychology through the Eyes of Faith* (San Francisco: HarperSanFrancisco, 1987).

69. On the complaints, see Minutes of the Board of Directors, Christian College Coalition, 8–9 May 1988, 2.

70. Eugene Habecker, "Proposal to the Board of Directors, Christian College Coalition," August 1985, 1–3; idem., telephone interview by author, 13 April 2000; and Minutes of the Board of Directors, Christian College Coalition, 11–12 September 1985, 3–4.

71. "Coalition Fellow Named," *Christian College News*, November 1986, 5.

72. "New Image for Coalition Promotes Enduring Values," *Christian College News*, April 1987, 1.

73. Minutes of the Board of Directors, Christian College Coalition, 27–28 September 1987, 5. By this time, Habecker was serving as board chairman.

74. Minutes of Telephone Conference Call, Board of Directors, Christian College Coalition, 30 November 1987, 1–5. See also Minutes, 31 January–1 February 1988, 3–4.

75. Quoted in "New Facilities Acquired on Capitol Hill," *The News*, January 1988, 1.

76. Daniel R. Chamberlain, "The Christian College Coalition: A View of the Future," address at Coalition annual meeting, 4–5 February 1986, photocopy sent to author.

77. Longman, "Celebrating Twenty Years of Service," 4–5; and "Statement of Revenue & Expenses—General Fund for the Years Ending June 30, 1988 and 1987," Christian College Coalition.

78. "Myron Augsburger Appointed Coalition President," *The News*, March 1988, 1. For insights on the CCCU as a movement, I am indebted to John A. Bernbaum, interview.

Chapter 5

1. Myron S. Augsburger, telephone interview by author, 29 January 2000; and "Myron Augsburger Appointed Coalition President," *The News*, March 1988, 1.

2. "Augsburger Appointed Coalition President," 1; Myron S. Augsburger, telephone interview by author, 8 June 2000; and Richard L. Gathro, interview by author, 27 January 2000, Washington, D.C.

3. Augsburger, telephone interview, 29 January 2000.

4. Robert C. Andringa, memorandum to Myron A. Augsburger, 12 May 1991, 3, CCCU archives, Washington, D.C. Andringa, who succeeded Augsburger to the Coalition presidency in 1994, then headed CEO Services Group, a consulting firm.

5. Myron S. Augsburger, Harrisonburg, Va., letter to the author, 27 July 2000.

6. Nicholas Wolterstorff, "The Mission of the Christian College at the End of the Twentieth Century," *Reformed Journal* 33 (June 1983): 17.

7. "Myron Augsburger Appointed Coalition President," *The News*, March 1988, 1.

8. "Presidents Gather for 1993 Annual Meeting," *The News*, March 1993, 3.

9. Alvin O. Austin, interview by author, 31 January 2000, Washington, D.C.

10. Myron S. Augsburger, "Beyond Evangelicalism: Seven Observations," *Perspectives*, n.d., 1–4. The Coalition published *Perspectives* on an occasional basis.

11. George K. Brushaber, interview by author, 1 February 2000, Washington, D.C.

12. See press release, Christian College Coalition, 28 September 1989, 1; David K. Winter, "NAICU Board Meeting Report," *The News*, January 1992, 2; and "Government Relations," *The Christian College Coalition: 1993 in Review*, 2.

13. Membership data was gathered from selected issues of *The News* between 1988 and 1994.

14. On membership criteria, see Minutes of the Board of Directors, Christian College Coalition, 11–12 September 1988; and 31 January–1 February 1993, 1–3.

15. Myron S. Augsburger, "President's Report," Board of Directors Meeting, Christian College Coalition, January 1994, 3–4.

16. Gathro, interview; and "Coalition Staff Expands," *The News*, July 1988, 3. On Goodrich's retirement from the Coalition, see "Coalition Staff Update," *The Christian College Coalition: 1990 in Review*, 1.

17. "Fall Students Christen Coalition's New Facilities," and "Wessner and Hatfield to Co-Chair Campaign," *The News*, October 1988, 1–2.

18. "Coalition Receives Largest Foundation Grant to Date," *The News*, November 1988, 1–2.

19. "Major Grants Received," *The Christian College Coalition: 1988 in Review*, 2.

20. "New Coalition Facilities Named 'The Dellenback Center,'" *The News*, March 1989, 1. On renovation costs of the townhouse, see Minutes of the Board of Directors, Christian College Coalition, 30 April–1 May, 1989, 5.

21. "Capital Campaign in the 'Homestretch,'" *The News*, August/September 1989, 4; "Murdock Trust Awards Grant as Campaign Deadline Nears," *The News*, December 1989, 1; and "Capital Campaign Nears Goal," *The Christian College Coalition: 1989 in Review*, 1.

22. "Prospectus for 8th Street Acquisitions," Christian College Coalition, 29 January 1990, CCCU archives, Washington, D.C.

23. "Coalition and ASP Offices Merge," *The News*, February 1990, 3; and "Coalition Friends Gather for Dellenback Center Dedication," *The News*, May 1990, 1.

24. All the following were published by HarperSanFrancisco as part of the Coalition's Supplemental Textbook Series: Susan V. Gallagher and Roger Lundin, *Literature through the Eyes of Faith* (1989); Richard T. Wright, *Biology through the Eyes of Faith* (1989); Ronald A. Wells, *History through the Eyes of Faith* (1989); Richard C. Chewning, John W. Eby, and Shirley J. Roels, *Business through Eyes of Faith* (1990); David A. Fraser and Tony Campolo, *Sociology through the Eyes of Faith* (1992); and Harold M. Best, *Music through the Eyes of Faith* (1993).

25. Karen A. Longman, "Celebrating Twenty Years of Service, 1976–1996," unpublished manuscript, 4, CCCU archives, Washington, D.C.

26. Information on these changes came from Gathro, interview; and from "Jerry Herbert Appointed Director of American Studies Program," *The News*, February 1992, 2. On the enrollment milestone, see "ASP Admits 1000th Student," *The News*, February 1989, 1.

27. Steven S. Garber, interview by author, 22 March 2000, Jackson, Tenn.; and idem., *The Fabric of Faithfulness: Weaving together Belief and Behavior during the University Years* (Downers Grove, Ill.: InterVarsity, 1996).

28. "Coalition Seeks New Director," *The News*, November 1988, 1–2; and "LASP Produces Lasting Effects," *The News*, February 1989, 1.

29. "New LASP Director Appointed," *The News*, May 1989, 1–2.

30. "New Director Appointed for Latin American Studies Program," *The News*, July 1990, 1; "Latin American Studies Program Flourishes in Costa Rica," *The Christian College Coalition: 1991 in Review*, 2; "Latin American Studies Program Adds Natural Science Track,"

The Christian College Coalition: 1992 in Review, 2; "LASP Announces Business Track," *The News*, March 1994, 2; and Council for Christian Colleges & Universities, *Guide to Off-Campus Study Programs*, 1999–2001 ed. (Washington, D.C.: CCCU, 1999), 133.

31. For example, see Minutes of the Board of Directors, Christian College Coalition, 11–12 September 1988, 2.

32. "Workshop for New Faculty Explores Educational Foundations," *The News*, July 1990, 2; and "First Regional Faculty Workshop Addresses the Use of Scripture in Teaching the Liberal Arts," *The News*, November 1993, 1.

33. Minutes of the Board of Directors, Christian College Coalition, 11–12 September 1988, 6.

34. "Diverse Christians Discuss 'Our Common Future,'" *The News*, January 1991, 2.

35. On the think tanks conducted in America, see "Hauerwas Think Tank Probes Living Out Truth in Society," *The News*, February 1991, 1; "Newbigin Think Tank Addresses the Gospel in a Pluralist Society," *The News*, July 1991, 3; "Carl F. H. Henry Leads Third Coalition Think Tank," *The News*, March 1992, 5; "Guinness Leads 5th CCC Think Tank," *The News*, February 1993, 2; and "Coalition Think Tank Explores Developing a Theology of Inclusion," *The News*, February 1994, 1.

36. Wesley K. Willmer, *Friends, Funds and Freshmen for Christian Colleges: A Manager's Guide to Advancing Resource Development* (Washington, D.C.: Christian College Coalition, 1987).

37. "Lilly Endowment Approves Coalition Study Grant," *The News*, July 1989, 1.

38. Wesley K. Willmer, ed., *Friends, Funds and Freshmen: A Management Guide to Christian College Advancement* (Washington, D.C.: Christian College Coalition, 1990). The third edition was published as *Advancing Christian Higher Education: A Guide to Effective Resource Development* (Washington, D.C.: Coalition for Christian Colleges & Universities, 1996).

39. "Lilly Endowment, Inc.," *The Christian College Coalition: 1990 in Review*, 2; and "Rebekah Basinger Hired to Direct Lilly Project," *The News*, July 1991, 2.

40. "Lilly Project Ends with a Flourish," *The News*, June 1994, 2. On the workshops, see "Lilly Project Flourishes," *The Christian College Coalition: 1992 in Review*, 1; and "Women in Christian College Fundraising Open a Dialogue," *The News*, January 1994, 1.

41. Minutes of the Board of Directors, Christian College Coalition, 29–30 January 1989, 5; "Major Foundation Grants Received," *The Christian College Coalition: 1989 in Review*, 2; and "Minority Concerns Task Force Meets in Philadelphia," *The News*, April 1990, 3.

42. D. John Lee, Alvaro L. Nieves, and Henry L. Allen, eds., *Ethnic-Minorities and Evangelical Christian Colleges* (Lanham, Md.: University Press of America/Christian College Coalition, 1991). See also Christine Lehmann, "Christian Colleges: Few Gains for Minorities," *Christianity Today*, 11 November 1991, 54.

43. "Minority Concerns Project Director Chosen to Help Colleges Reflect World's Diversity," *The News*, January 1992, 1.

44. For overviews of the ORED project, see "From the Director's Desk," *The Open Door* (Fall 1992): 1; "Racial/Ethnic Diversity Initiative Enters Second Year," *The Christian College Coalition: 1992 in Review*, 1; and "Office of Racial/Ethnic Diversity," *The Christian College Coalition: 1993 in Review*, 1.

45. Information on the end of the project came from Myron S. Augsburger, "Diversity—Our Challenge," *The Open Door* (Spring/Summer 1994): 1, 6; idem., telephone interview, 29 January 2000; Gathro, interview; and "Diversity Initiatives," *The Christian College Coalition: 1994 in Review*, 1.

46. Carl H. Lundquist, "Report of the President," Christian College Consortium, 16 October 1989, 5–6.

47. John A. Bernbaum, memorandum to Myron S. Augsburger, 1 September 1989, 1–2, CCCU archives, Washington, D.C.

48. Minutes of the Board of Directors, Christian College Coalition, 10–11 September 1989, 5.

49. R. Judson Carlberg, interview by author, 1 February 2000, Washington, D.C.

50. Minutes of the Board of Directors, Christian College Coalition, 28–29 January 1990, 4. These minutes include business transacted by telephone the previous month.

51. "Director Appointed for Coalition's Los Angeles Film Studies Center," *The News*, September 1990, 1 and 3.

52. "Coalition's New Los Angeles Film Studies Center Ready for Action," *The News*, January 1991, 1; and "L.A. Film Studies Center in Full Swing," *The News*, August/September 1991, 1 and 3.

53. "Film and the Christian: The Los Angeles Film Studies Center Offers New Perspectives," *The News*, December 1992, 1.

54. CCCU, *Guide to Off-Campus Study Programs*, 1999–2001 ed., 88.

55. "Harvey Fellowship Program Assists Graduate Students," *The Christian College Coalition: 1991 in Review*, 2; "Pew Funds Social Welfare Project," *The News*, June 1992, 2; and "Women's Conference Addresses Gender Issues in Higher Education," *The News*, April 1993, 3.

56. "Global Connections" became a regular column in *The News* starting with the May 1990 issue.

57. "Soviet Initiatives Project Builds Bridges, Opens Opportunities," *The News*, May 1990, 4.

58. "Soviet Officials Explore Spiritual Values in Higher Education," *The News*, November 1990, special section, 1–4.

59. Ibid., 3.

60. "Soviet Initiatives Project Builds Educational Bridges," *The Christian College Coalition: 1990 in Review*, 1.

61. Myron S. Augsburger, Harrisonburg, Va., letter to the author, 27 July 2000.

62. See "New MBA Curriculum Will Bring the Free Market to Russian Classrooms," *The News*, November 1991, 1, 3; and "Russian-American MBA Curriculum Is in Use!" *Russia Link* (Spring 1993): 6.

63. On the progress of the RSP, see "New 'Russian Initiative' Expands and Builds on the Foundation of 1990–92 Pilot Project," *Russia Link* (Fall 1992): 1; "Coalition Hires Russian Studies Program Director," *The News*, July/August 1993, 1, 5; and "Russian Studies Program Readies for Take-Off," *Russia Link* (Fall 1993): 1.

64. John A. Bernbaum, interview by author, 1 February 2000, Washington, D.C.; "Russian-American Christian University Project Gains Momentum," *Russia Link* (Fall 1993): 2–3; Minutes of the Board of Directors, Christian College Coalition, 30–31 January 1994, 4; and Beverly Nickles, "Christian Liberal Arts Program Blossoms in Moscow," *Christianity Today*, 20 May 1996, 73.

65. "Bernbaum Receives Russian Doctorate," *Russia Link* (Spring 1995): 3.

66. "Christian College Coalition Announces New Oxford Summer Study Program," *The News*, November 1990, 1, 3; Minutes of the Board of Directors, Christian College Coalition, 13–14 October 1991, 2; and CCCU, *Guide to Off-Campus Study Programs*, 1999–2001 ed., 217–30.

67.Karen A. Longman, interview by author, 25 March 2000, Greenville, Ill.; "Coalition Launches New Middle East Studies Program in Cairo, Egypt," *The News*, February 1993, 1; "Middle East Studies Program Launched in Cairo amid Historic Happenings," *The News*, October 1993, 1; and CCCU, *Guide to Off-Campus Programs*, 1999–2001 ed., 152.

68. "Coalition President Announces Plans for Personal Transition in Work and Ministry," *The News*, September 1993, 1.

69. Randy Frame, "Theological Drift: Christian Higher Ed the Culprit?" *Christianity Today*, 9 April 1990, 43, 46. This article reported on a seminar in Pittsburgh that in part was provoked by Hunter's book, *Evangelicalism: The Coming Generation* (Chicago: University of Chicago, 1987).

70. "Statements of Financial Position," and "Statements of Activities," Christian College Coalition, 30 June 1994 and 1993.

71. Austin, interview.

Chapter 6

1. Robert C. Andringa, interview by author, 27 January 2000, Vienna, Va.; Alvin O. Austin, interview by author, 31 January 2000, Washington, D.C; "Robert C. Andringa Named Head of Christian College Coalition," *The News*, March 1994, 1; and "Into the Future: Andringa Takes the Coalition Helm," *The News*, September 1994, 1.

2. Andringa, interview, 27 January 2000.

3. Robert C. Andringa, telephone interview by author, 26 June 2000.

4. Andringa, interview, 27 January 2000; and "Robert C. Andringa Named Head of Christian College Coalition," 1.

5. Robert C. Andringa, "Relevance, Quality and Unity—Our Three Guiding Themes," *The News*, September 1994, 2.

6. "Staff Reorganization," *The Christian College Coalition: 1994 in Review*, 1; and Jay L. Kesler, interview by author, 1 February 2000, Washington, D.C. A further adjustment came in 1998 when Andringa promoted Gathro to senior vice president, giving him more management responsibilities. See "Staff Updates and Additions," *The News*, November 1998, 4.

7. Regarding the retreat, see Robert C. Andringa, "Coalition Board Takes Significant Steps at October Retreat," *The News*, November/December 1994, 2. On the Racial Harmony Council, see "Sharing Struggles and Celebrating Progress toward Diversity," *The News*, January 1995, 1.

8. Andringa, interview, 27 January 2000; idem, "Coalition Board Takes Significant Steps at October Retreat," 2; and "In with the New Name, Out with the Old . . . ," *The News*, March 1995, 1.

9. Robert C. Andringa, "A New Name and New Friends for the Coalition," *The News*, February 1995, 2; and CCCU, *Directory and Resource Guide for Christian Higher Education, 1999–2000* (Washington, D.C.: Council for Christian Colleges & Universities, 1999), 247–82.

10. Information on membership came from various issues of *The News*. On membership criteria and the mission statement, see Minutes of the Board of Directors, Coalition for Christian Colleges & Universities, 15–18 July 1995, 3; and 2–5 February 1997, 4.

11. "Volunteers Provide Leadership for CCCU," *The News*, November/December 1996, 2; and "Volunteer Leaders," Council for Christian Colleges & Universities, 13 January 2000, photocopy of list provided at 2000 annual meeting.

12. George K. Brushaber, interview by author, 1 February 2000, Washington, D.C.

13. Robert C. Andringa, "Ten Challenges for Trustees and Leaders of CCCU Campuses," January 2000, 2, photocopy given to author.

14. Andringa, interview, 27 January 2000; "Andringa Active in Government Relations," *The News*, September/October 1995, 1; "High Priority on Federal Relations," *Coalition for Christian Colleges & Universities: 1995 Year in Review*, 1–2; and "Fall Program Briefs: Washington Higher Education Secretariat," *The News*, November 1998, 1.

15. "Board Approves New Student Journalism Program," *The News*, January/February 1996, 3; and "Coalition to Host Summer Institute of Journalism," *The News*, May/June 1996, 1.

16. Minutes of the Board of Directors, Coalition for Christian Colleges & Universities, 26–29 July 1997, 2; "Two New Student Programs Announced," *The News*, November 1997, 1, 3; "Hosts Hold Dedication for Oxford Honors Program," *The News*, February 1999, 2; and "Student Programs See Leadership Changes," *The News*, September/October 1999, 2–3.

17. "Student Programs See Leadership Changes," 2–3; and "China Studies Program Names First Director, Secures Host University," *The News*, November 1998, 2.

18. "Council Members Participation in CCCU Student Programs," CCCU chart, photocopy given to author; Margery S. Bernbaum, interview by author, 1 February 2000, Washington, D.C.; and CCCU, *Directory and Resource Guide for Christian Higher Education, 1999–2000*, 17–26.

19. Andringa, email to author, 4 September 2000; and Richard Gathro, email to author, 18 September 2000.

20. "First Presidents' Dialogues," *Coalition for Christian Colleges & Universities: 1995 Year in Review*, 3.

21. David S. Dockery, interview by author, 16 March 2000, Jackson, Tenn.; Carla Sanderson, interview by author, 14 March 2000, Jackson, Tenn.; "Presidents' Institute," *The News*, September 1996, 1; "ELDI: Past and Future Events," *The News*, September/October 1999, 3; and the CCCU's Women's Leadership Initiative brochure.

22. "Murdock Trust Awards Faculty Development Grant," *The News*, April 1996, 2–3; "*Communication through the Eyes of Faith* Volume to be Published," *The News*, March 1996, 1.

23. "Mission Statement," *Quaerens*, June 1999, 2. See also "How It All Began," *Quaerens*, June 1999, 1–2. *Quaerens* is the newsletter of the seminar project.

24. Harold Heie, telephone interview by author, 30 March 2000; "CCCU Receives Three Grants Totaling $1.4 Million," *The News*, September/October 1999, 2; and "CCCU 1999 Initiative Grants Announced," *The News*, December 1999, 2.

25. "CCCU Names New Vice President for Professional Development & Research," *The News*, December 1999, 1; and "CCCU Campus-Based Faculty Development Program" [news item online]; available from http://www.cccu.org/projects/facdev/; Internet; accessed 16 June 2000.

26. "Stewardship Project," *Coalition for Christian Colleges & Universities: 1995 Year in Review*, 2; "Global Stewardship Conference," *The News*, April 1996, 1; and Minutes of the Board of Directors, Coalition for Christian Colleges & Universities, 2–5 February 1997, 3.

27. D. John Lee and Gloria Goris Stronks, eds., *Assessment of Christian Higher Education: Rhetoric and Reality* (Lanham, Md.: University Press of America, 1994).

28. "Coalition Research Journal Published," *The News*, October 1994, 3.

29. "Assessment at Christian Colleges: How are We Doing?" *The News*, November/December 1994, 1.

30. Karen A. Longman, interview by author, 25 March 2000, Greenville, Ill.; and L. Katherine Robbin, "Colleges That Take Values Seriously: Christian Colleges Initiate a New Study to Measure Effects of a Faith-Based Education," *Christianity Today*, 16 November 1998, 92–105 [advertising section].

31. "FIPSE Findings at the Center of Our Focus," *FIPSE—Through the Eyes of Faculty*, October 1999, 6.

32. Karen A. Longman, "Envisioning the Future of the Christian University," in *The Future of Christian Higher Education*, eds. David S. Dockery and David P. Gushee (Nashville: Broadman & Holman, 1999), 46–48.

33. Longman, interview; and Minutes of the Board of Directors, Coalition for Christian Colleges & Universities, 2–5 February 1997, 3.

34. "Quality Retention: What We Are Learning," *The News*, January/February 1998, 3–4; and Christine J. Gardner, "Keeping Students in School: Christian Colleges Seek to Improve Retention Rate," *Christianity Today*, 7 September 1998, 34–38.

35. L. Katherine Robbin, "Christian Colleges' Happy Customers: Higher Education is Taking Seriously the Needs and Interests of Students," *Christianity Today*, 1 March 1999, 75–88 [advertising section]; "Kicking Off Year III: 'Affirming Students' Strengths in the Critical Years,'" *CCCU Quality Retention Project*, September 1999, 1–2; and Ronald P. Mahurin, draft of CCCU Board Report, 24 June 2000, 2, photocopy sent to author.

36. "'Faithful Change' Project Launched," *The News*, November 1998, 2, 4; "Faithful Change: Promoting Spiritual Development in College Students," CCCU Research Proposal to the John Templeton Foundation, 9 August 1999, photocopy given to author by Karen Longman; and Mahurin, draft of CCCU Board Report, 24 June 2000, 1, photocopy sent to author.

37. "The Coalition and the World Wide Web," *The News*, November/December 1995, 2; "Christian Education and the World Wide Web," *The News*, January/February 1996, 1; and "christiancollege.org," *The News*, November 1998, 4.

38. "Collaborative Distance Learning," *The News*, November 1997, 1. For board approval, see Minutes of the Board of Directors, Coalition for Christian Colleges & Universities, 6–7 February 1998, 2.

39. "Christian University GlobalNet," *The News*, November 1998, 4; and "Christian University GlobalNet Is Launched," *The News*, February 1999, 3.

40. "Christian University GlobalNet Update," *The News*, November/December 1999, 3; and "Christian University GlobalNet: 1999 Highlights," report distributed at CCCU annual meeting, 30 January–1 February, 2000.

41. Gaylen J. Byker, interview by author, 7 July 1999, Grand Rapids, Mich.; and Joel A. Carpenter, interview by author, 9 July 1999, Grand Rapids, Mich.

42. Andringa, email to author, 4 September 2000.

43. Andringa, interview, 27 January 2000; "New Era Foundation Loss," *Coalition for Christian Colleges & Universities: 1995 Year in Review*, 1; and Minutes of the Board of Directors, Coalition for Christian Colleges & Universities, 20 September 1995, 1–2. A recovery of 88 percent was noted in Minutes of the Board of Directors, Coalition for Christian Colleges & Universities, 5 November 1998, 1.

44. "Pro-Active Media Relations," *Coalition for Christian Colleges & Universities: 1995 Year in Review*, 2.

45. Robert C. Andringa, "A Campaign in the Making," *The News*, October 1996, 2; and Minutes of the Board of Directors, Coalition for Christian Colleges & Universities, 27–30 July 1996, 1–2.

46. Robert C. Andringa, "Four Priorities for Prayer and Planning," *The News*, April 1997, 2; "Search: CCCU Communications Director," *The News*, January/February 1997, 2; "New to the CCCU Staff," *The News*, Summer 1997, 4; "The United Fund," *The News*, November 1997, 1; and Andringa, email to author, 4 September 2000.

47. "First 'National Forum' Makes Coalition History," *The News*, May 1998, 1–2; Gordon Van Harn, interview by author, 7 July 1999, Grand Rapids, Mich.; and "CCCU Events," *The News*, December 1999, 3.

48. "CCCU Members Receive up to $10 Million in Scholarship Aid," *The News*, May 1998, 2; and Robert C. Andringa, memorandum to Dick West and Craig Hammond of Westwood Foundation, 4 May 1998, 1–2, CCCU archives, Washington, D.C.

49. "CCCU Receives Its Largest Grant Ever," *The News*, May 1998, 2–3; and "Coalition to Break Ground on New Building," *The News*, November 1998, 1. I personally observed some of the last phase of construction in January 2000.

50. Andringa, "It's More Than a Name Change," *The News*, April/May 1999, 3.

51. "CCCU Introduces New Logo," *The News*, April/May 1999, 1; and "Christian Higher Education Month," *The News*, September/October 1999, 1.

52. Leo Reisberg, "Enrollments Surge at Christian Colleges," *Chronicle of Higher Education*, 5 March 1999, A42–44.

53. *Volunteer Leader News*, March 2000, 1–2. Kevin Trowbridge, formerly director of marketing at Union University, succeeded Peterson as the CCCU's director of communications during the summer of 2000. Robert C. Andringa, email to author, 22 July 2000.

54. *Volunteer Leader News*, March 2000, 1–2; and Andringa, emails to author, 25 June 2000 and 4 September 2000. The first volume in the new Baker imprint is Quentin J. Schultze, *Communicating for Life: Christian Stewardship in Community and Media* (Grand Rapids: Baker Books, 2000), which was originally intended for the Supplemental Textbook Series as *Communication through the Eyes of Faith*.

55. Statistics came from Rich Gathro's oral report at the CCCU annual meeting, 31 January 2000; and Andringa, email, 25 June 2000. On membership, see the appendix.

56. Karen A. Longman, "Celebrating Twenty Years of Service, 1976–1996," unpublished manuscript, 8, CCCU archives, Washington, D.C.; and idem., interview.

57. John A. Bernbaum, interview by author, 1 February 2000, Washington, D.C.

58. Mark A. Noll, *The Scandal of the Evangelical Mind* (Grand Rapids: Eerdmans, 1994).

59. See Joel A. Carpenter, "Sustaining Christian Intellectual Commitments: Lessons from the Recent Past," in *The Future of Christian Higher Education*, 105–19.

60. Brushaber, interview.

61. John R. Dellenback, telephone interview by author, 29 January 2000.

Suggested Readings on Christian Higher Education

Burtchaell, James Tunstead. *The Dying of the Light: The Disengagement of Colleges and Universities from Their Christian Churches*. Grand Rapids: Eerdmans, 1998.

Carpenter, Joel A., and Kenneth W. Shipps, eds. *Making Higher Education Christian: The History and Mission of Evangelical Colleges in America*. Grand Rapids: Christian University Press/Eerdmans, 1987.

Cunninggim, Merrimon. *Uneasy Partners: The College and the Church*. Nashville: Abingdon, 1994.

De Jong, Arthur J. *Reclaiming a Mission: New Directions for the Church-Related College*. Grand Rapids: Eerdmans, 1990.

Diekema, Anthony J. *Academic Freedom and Christian Scholarship*. Grand Rapids: Eerdmans, 2000.

Dockery, David S., and David P. Gushee, eds. *The Future of Christian Higher Education*. Nashville: Broadman & Holman, 1999.

Fisher, Ben C. *The Idea of a Christian University in Today's World*. Macon, Ga.: Mercer, 1989.

Gill, David W., ed. *Should God Get Tenure? Essays on Religion and Higher Education*. Grand Rapids: Eerdmans, 1997.

Gleason, Philip. *Contending with Modernity: Catholic Higher Education in the Twentieth Century*. New York: Oxford, 1995.

Heie, Harold, and David L. Wolfe, eds. *The Reality of Christian Learning: Strategies for Faith-Discipline Integration.* Grand Rapids: Christian University Press/Eerdmans, 1987.

———. *Slogans or Distinctives: Reforming Christian Higher Education.* Lanham, Md.: University Press of America, 1993.

Holmes, Arthur F. *The Idea of a Christian College.* Revised ed. Grand Rapids: Eerdmans, 1987.

———. *Shaping Character: Moral Education in the Christian College.* Grand Rapids: Eerdmans, 1991.

Hughes, Richard T., and William B. Adrian, eds. *Models for Christian Higher Education: Strategies for Survival and Success in the Twenty-First Century.* Grand Rapids: Eerdmans, 1997.

Mannoia, V. James. *Christian Liberal Arts: An Education That Goes Beyond.* Lanham, Md.: Rowman & Littlefield, 2000.

Marsden, George M. *The Soul of the American University: From Protestant Establishment to Established Nonbelief.* New York: Oxford, 1994.

———. *The Outrageous Idea of Christian Scholarship.* New York: Oxford, 1997.

Noll, Mark A. *The Scandal of the Evangelical Mind.* Grand Rapids: Eerdmans, 1994.

Ramm, Bernard L. *The Christian College in the Twentieth Century.* Grand Rapids: Eerdmans, 1963.

Ringenberg, William C. *The Christian College: A History of Protestant Higher Education in America.* Grand Rapids: Christian University Press/Eerdmans, 1984.

Sandin, Robert T. *The Search for Excellence: The Christian College in an Age of Educational Competition.* Macon, Ga.: Mercer, 1982.

Sloan, Douglas. *Faith and Knowledge: Mainline Protestantism and American Higher Education.* Louisville: Westminster/John Knox, 1994.

Wells, Ronald A., ed. *Keeping Faith: Embracing the Tensions in Christian Higher Education.* Grand Rapids: Eerdmans, 1996.

Appendix

Members and Affiliates of the Council for Christian Colleges & Universities as of August 1, 2000.

Members	Year Admitted
Abilene Christian University (Texas)	1995
Anderson University (Indiana)	1982
Asbury College (Kentucky)	1976
Azusa Pacific University (California)	1976
Bartlesville Wesleyan College (Oklahoma)	1978
Belhaven College (Mississippi)	1979
Bethel College (Indiana)	1984
Bethel College (Kansas)	1980
Bethel College (Minnesota)	1976
Biola University (California)	1976
Bluffton College (Ohio)	1991
Bryan College (Tennessee)	1976
California Baptist University (California)	1990
Calvin College (Michigan)	1981
Campbell University (North Carolina)	1979
Campbellsville University (Kentucky)	1976
Cedarville University (Ohio)	1991
College of the Ozarks (Missouri)	1996
Colorado Christian University (Colorado)	1985
Cornerstone University (Michigan)	1991

Members	Year Admitted
Covenant College (Georgia)	1976
Crichton College (Tennessee)	2000
Dallas Baptist University (Texas)	1984
Dordt College (Iowa)	1981
East Texas Baptist University (Texas)	1995
Eastern College (Pennsylvania)	1976
Eastern Mennonite University (Virginia)	1976
Eastern Nazarene College (Massachusetts)	1982
Erskine College (South Carolina)	1991
Evangel University (Missouri)	1976
Fresno Pacific University (California)	1981
Geneva College (Pennsylvania)	1976
George Fox University (Oregon)	1976
Gordon College (Massachusetts)	1976
Goshen College (Indiana)	1985
Grace College and Seminary (Indiana)	1976
Grand Canyon University (Arizona)	1981
Greenville College (Illinois)	1976
Hope International University (California)	1994
Houghton College (New York)	1976
Houston Baptist University (Texas)	2000
Howard Payne University (Texas)	2000
Huntington College (Indiana)	1978
Indiana Wesleyan University (Indiana)	1976
John Brown University (Arkansas)	1976
Judson College (Alabama)	2000
Judson College (Illinois)	1976
Kentucky Christian College (Kentucky)	1999
King College (Tennessee)	1979
The King's University College (Alberta)	1987
Lee University (Tennessee)	1981
LeTourneau University (Texas)	1985
Lipscomb University (Tennessee)	1999
Malone College (Ohio)	1976
The Master's College and Seminary (California)	1978
Messiah College (Pennsylvania)	1976
Mid-America Nazarene University (Kansas)	1978
Milligan College (Tennessee)	1984

Members	Year Admitted
Montreat College (North Carolina)	1989
Mount Vernon Nazarene College (Ohio)	1982
North Greenville College (South Carolina)	2000
North Park University (Illinois)	1981
Northwest Christian College (Oregon)	1981
Northwest College (Washington)	1992
Northwest Nazarene University (Idaho)	1979
Northwestern College (Iowa)	1978
Northwestern College (Minnesota)	1980
Nyack College (New York)	1976
Oklahoma Baptist University (Oklahoma)	1994
Oklahoma Christian University (Oklahoma)	1998
Olivet Nazarene University (Illinois)	1978
Oral Roberts University (Oklahoma)	1997
Palm Beach Atlantic College (Florida)	1982
Point Loma Nazarene University (California)	1979
Redeemer College (Ontario)	1986
Roberts Wesleyan College (New York)	1982
Seattle Pacific University (Washington)	1976
Simpson College (California)	1976
Southern Nazarene University (Oklahoma)	1978
Southern Wesleyan University (South Carolina)	1978
Southwest Baptist University (Missouri)	1995
Spring Arbor College (Michigan)	1978
Sterling College (Kansas)	1980
Tabor College (Kansas)	1979
Taylor University (Indiana)	1976
Trevecca Nazarene University (Tennessee)	1980
Trinity Christian College (Illinois)	1980
Trinity International University (Illinois)	1976
Trinity Western University (British Columbia)	1986
Union University (Tennessee)	1993
University of Sioux Falls (South Dakota)	1981
Vanguard University of Southern California (California)	1981
Warner Pacific College (Oregon)	1982
Warner Southern College (Florida)	1982

Members	Year Admitted
Western Baptist College (Oregon)	1992
Westmont College (California)	1976
Wheaton College (Illinois)	1976
Whitworth College (Washington)	1981
William Tyndale College (Michigan)	1998
Williams Baptist College (Arkansas)	1994

Affiliates	Year Admitted
Atlantic Baptist University (Canada)	1995
Bethune-Cookman College (Florida)	1997
Bible College of New Zealand (New Zealand)	2000
Briercrest Bible College (Canada)	2000
Central Baptist College (Arkansas)	1995
Chongshin University and Theological Seminary (South Korea)	1996
Christ's College (Taiwan)	1999
Columbia International University (South Carolina)	2000
Crestmont College (California)	2000
The Criswell College (Texas)	1995
Crown College (Minnesota)	1997
Cumberland College (Kentucky)	1999
Dallas Theological Seminary (Texas)	1999
Denver Seminary (Colorado)	1998
Emmanuel College (Georgia)	2000
European Nazarene Bible College (Switzerland)	2000
Franciscan University of Steubenville (Ohio)	1996
Fuller Theological Seminary (California)	1996
Hoseo University (South Korea)	2000
Institute for Christian Studies (Canada)	1998
The International University (Austria)	1995
Jerusalem University College (Israel)	1998
Lithuania Christian Fund College (Lithuania)	1997
North American Baptist College/ Edmonton Baptist Seminary (Canada)	1999
North Central University (Minnesota)	1996
Norwegian Teacher Academy (Norway)	1997

Affiliates	Year Admitted
Oakwood College (Alabama)	1999
Philadelphia College of Bible (Pennsylvania)	1996
Providence College and Seminary (Canada)	1996
Reformed Bible College (Michigan)	1999
Regent University (Virginia)	1995
Russian-American Christian University (Russia)	1997
St. Petersburg Christian University (Russia)	1999
Seoul Women's University (South Korea)	2000
Sheng-te Christian College (Taiwan)	2000
Southeastern College (Florida)	1999
Southwestern Baptist Theological Seminary (Texas)	1996
Taylor University (Fort Wayne campus [Indiana])	1996
Tokyo Christian University (Japan)	1995
Tyndale College and Seminary (Canada)	1997
Uganda Christian University (Uganda)	2000
Universidad Evangélica Boliviana (Bolivia)	1996
Waynesburg College (Pennsylvania)	1997
Wesley Institute for Ministry and the Arts (Australia)	2000

CCCU Board Chairs

Name (Institution)	Year(s)
Richard Chase (Biola University)	1976–79
Daniel Weiss (Eastern College)	1979–81
Lon Randall (Malone College)	1981
David Winter (Westmont College)	1981–83
Friedhelm Radandt (Northwestern College, Iowa)	1983–85
Daniel Chamberlain (Houghton College)	1985–86
Anthony Diekema (Calvin College)	1986–87
Eugene Habecker (Huntington College)	1987–88
Clyde Cook (Biola University)	1988–89
Jay Kesler (Taylor University)	1989–91
David LeShana (Seattle Pacific University)	1991
Donald Ericksen (Northwestern College, Minnesota)	1991–93

Name (Institution)	Years
Alvin Austin (LeTourneau University)	1993–95
Arthur Self (Seattle Pacific University)	1995
Judson Carlberg (Gordon College)	1995–97
James Bultman (Northwestern College, Iowa)	1997–99
Royce Money (Abilene Christian University)	1999–2001
Loren Gresham (Southern Nazarene University)	2001–

For current information on the members, affiliates, programs, and services of the Council for Christian College & Universities, please see their website:

www.cccu.org

James A. Patterson received his Ph.D. from Princeton Theological Seminary. He has written numerous articles, has contributed to several books, and has also published a history of Mid-America Baptist Theological Seminary titled *To All the World*. He currently serves as professor of Christian studies at Union University in Jackson, Tennessee.